England, A Nation In Verse

Poetry is a fascinating use of language. With almost a million words at its command it is not surprising that these Isles have produced some of the most beautiful, moving and descriptive verse through the centuries. In this series we look at a particular Nation through the eyes and minds of our most gifted poets to bring you a unique poetic guide.

The English language has grown into the Worlds pre-dominant spoken language. It's sources are rich and diverse, absorbing from other cultures and times without hesitation. It surely follows that when we add the talents of Shakespeare, Keats, Shelley, Kipling and Blake to a myriad of others that its beauty and reach entrance us with their thoughts and visions. In this volume of its greatest works these remarkable poems present a wonderful companion through the long heritage of the English Language and its poets.

Many of the poems are also available as an audiobook from our sister company Portable Poetry. Many samples are at our youtube channel http://www.youtube.com/user/PortablePoetry?feature=mhee The full volume can be purchased from iTunes, Amazon and other digital stores. Among the readers are Richard Mitchley and Ghizela Rowe

There Is Pleasure In The Pathless Woods by Lord Byron
She Walks In Beauty by Lord Byron
The Ship Of Death by DH Lawrence
Afternoon in School The Last Lesson by DH Lawrence

The Passionate Shepherd To His Love by Christopher Marlowe

Come live with me and be my love,
And we will all the pleasures prove
That valleys, groves, hills, and fields,
Woods, or steepy mountain yields.

And we will sit upon the rocks,
Seeing the shepherds feed their flocks,
By shallow rivers to whose falls
Melodious birds sing madrigals.

And I will make thee beds of roses
And a thousand fragrant posies,
A cap of flowers, and a kirtle
Embroidered all with leaves of myrtle;

A gown made of the finest wool
Which from our pretty lambs we pull;
Fair lined slippers for the cold,
With buckles of the purest gold;

A belt of straw and ivy buds,
With coral clasps and amber studs:
And if these pleasures may thee move,
Come live with me, and be my love.

The shepherds' swains shall dance and sing
For thy delight each May morning:
If these delights thy mind may move,
Then live with me and be my love.

The Face That Launched A Thousand Ships by Christopher Marlowe

Was this the face that launch'd a thousand ships,
And burnt the topless towers of Ilium?
Sweet Helen, make me immortal with a kiss.
Her lips suck forth my soul: see where it flies!
Come, Helen, come, give me my soul again.
Here will I dwell, for heaven is in these lips,
And all is dross that is not Helena.
I will be Paris, and for love of thee,
Instead of Troy, shall Wittenberg be sack'd;
And I will combat with weak Menelaus,
And wear thy colours on my plumed crest;
Yea, I will wound Achilles in the heel,

And then return to Helen for a kiss.
O, thou art fairer than the evening air
Clad in the beauty of a thousand stars;
Brighter art thou than flaming Jupiter
When he appear'd to hapless Semele;
More lovely than the monarch of the sky
In wanton Arethusa's azur'd arms;
And none but thou shalt be my paramour!

Shall I Compare Thee To A Summers Day by William Shakespeare

Thou art more lovely and more temperate:
Rough winds do shake the darling buds of May,
And summer's lease hath all too short a date:
Sometime too hot the eye of heaven shines,
And often is his gold complexion dimm'd;
And every fair from fair sometime declines,
By chance or nature's changing course untrimm'd;
But thy eternal summer shall not fade
Nor lose possession of that fair thou owest;
Nor shall Death brag thou wander'st in his shade,
When in eternal lines to time thou growest:
So long as men can breathe or eyes can see,
So long lives this and this gives life to thee.

Let Me Not To The Marriage Of True Minds by William Shakespeare

Let me not to the marriage of true minds
Admit impediments. Love is not love
Which alters when it alteration finds,
Or bends with the remover to remove:
Oh, no! it is an ever-fixéd mark,
That looks on tempests and is never shaken;
It is the star to every wandering bark,
Whose worth's unknown, although his height be taken.
Love's not time's fool, though rosy lips and cheeks
Within his bending sickle's compass come'
Love alters not with his brief hours and weeks,
But bears it out even to the edge of doom.
If this be error and upon me proved,
I never writ, nor no man ever loved.

To Celia by Ben Johnson

Drink to me only with thine eyes,
And I will pledge with mine;
Or leave a kiss but in the cup
And I'll not look for wine.
The thirst that from the soul doth rise
Doth ask a drink divine;
But might I of Jove's nectar sup,
I would not change for thine.

I sent thee late a rosy wreath,
Not so much honouring thee
As giving it a hope that there
It could not wither'd be;
But thou thereon didst only breathe,
And sent'st it back to me;
Since when it grows, and smells, I swear,
Not of itself but thee!

On My First Son by Ben Jonson

Farewell, thou child of my right hand, and joy;
My sin was too much hope of thee, lov'd boy.
Seven years thou wert lent to me, and I thee pay,
Exacted by thy fate, on the just day.
Oh, could I lose all father now ! For why
Will man lament the state he should envy?
To have so soon 'scaped world's and flesh's rage,
And if no other misery, yet age !
Rest in soft peace, and, asked, say, Here doth lie
Ben Jonson his best piece of poetry.
For whose sake henceforth all his vows be such
As what he loves may never like too much.

The Good Morrow by John Donne

I wonder by my troth, what thou and I
Did, till we loved ? were we not wean'd till then ?
But suck'd on country pleasures, childishly ?
Or snorted we in the Seven Sleepers' den ?
'Twas so ; but this, all pleasures fancies be;
If ever any beauty I did see,
Which I desired, and got, 'twas but a dream of thee.

And now good-morrow to our waking souls,
Which watch not one another out of fear;
For love all love of other sights controls,
And makes one little room an everywhere.
Let sea-discoverers to new worlds have gone ;
Let maps to other, worlds on worlds have shown;
Let us possess one world ; each hath one, and is one.

My face in thine eye, thine in mine appears,
And true plain hearts do in the faces rest;
Where can we find two better hemispheres
Without sharp north, without declining west ?
Whatever dies, was not mix'd equally;
If our two loves be one, or thou and I
Love so alike that none can slacken, none can die.

Witchcraft By A Picture by John Donne

I fix mine eye on thine, and there
Pity my picture burning in thine eye;
My picture drown'd in a transparent tear,
When I look lower I espy;
Hadst thou the wicked skill
By pictures made and marr'd, to kill,
How many ways mightst thou perform thy will?

But now I've drunk thy sweet salt tears,
And though thou pour more, I'll depart;
My picture vanished, vanish all fears
That I can be endamaged by that art;
Though thou retain of me
One picture more, yet that will be,
Being in thine own heart, from all malice free.

On Shakespeare by John Milton

What needs my Shakespeare for his honored bones
To labor of an age in piled stones,
Or that his hallowed relics should be hid
Under a star-ypointing pyramid?
Dear son of memory, great heir of fame,
What need'st thou such weak witness of thy name?
Thou in our wonder and astonishment
Hast built thyself a livelong monument.
For, whilst, to the shame of slow-endeavouring art,
Thy easy numbers flow, and that each heart
Hath from the leaves of thy unvalued book
Those Delphic lines with deep impression took,
Then thou our fancy of itself bereaving,
Dost make us marble with too much conceiving,
And so sepúlchred in such pomp dost lie
That kings for such a tomb would wish to die.

On The Morning Of Christs Nativity byJohn Milton

This is the month, and this the happy morn,
Wherein the Son of Heaven's eternal King,
Of wedded maid and Virgin Mother born,
Our great redemption from above did bring;
For so the holy sages once did sing,
That he our deadly forfeit should release,
And with his Father work us a perpetual peace.

II
That glorious Form, that Light unsufferable,
And that far-beaming blaze of majesty,
Wherewith he wont at Heaven's high council-table
To sit the midst of Trinal Unity,
He laid aside, and, here with us to be,

Forsook the Courts of everlasting Day,
And chose with us a darksome house of mortal clay.

III
Say, Heavenly Muse, shall not thy sacred vein
Afford a present to the Infant God?
Hast thou no verse, no hymn, or solemn strain,
To welcome him to this his new abode,
Now while the heaven, by the Sun's team untrod,
Hath took no print of the approaching light,
And all the spangled host keep watch in squadrons bright?

IV
See how from far upon the Eastern road
The star-led Wisards haste with odours sweet!
Oh! run; prevent them with thy humble ode,
And lay it lowly at his blessèd feet;
Have thou the honour first thy Lord to greet,
And join thy voice unto the Angel Quire,
From out his secret altar touched with hallowed fire.

The Hymn
I
It was the winter wild,
While the heaven-born child
All meanly wrapt in the rude manger lies;
Nature, in awe to him,
Had doffed her gaudy trim,
With her great Master so to sympathize:
It was no season then for her
To wanton with the Sun, her lusty Paramour.

II
Only with speeches fair
She woos the gentle air
To hide her guilty front with innocent snow,
And on her naked shame,
Pollute with sinful blame,
The saintly veil of maiden white to throw;
Confounded, that her Maker's eyes
Should look so near upon her foul deformities.

III
But he, her fears to cease,
Sent down the meek-eyed Peace:
She, crowned with olive green, came softly sliding
Down through the turning sphere,
His ready Harbinger,
With turtle wing the amorous clouds dividing;
And, waving wide her myrtle wand,
She strikes a universal peace through sea and land.

IV

No war, or battail's sound,
Was heard the world around;
The idle spear and shield were high uphung;
The hookèd chariot stood,
Unstained with hostile blood;
The trumpet spake not to the armèd throng;
And Kings sat still with awful eye,
As if they surely knew their sovran Lord was by.

V

But peaceful was the night
Wherein the Prince of Light
His reign of peace upon the earth began.
The winds, with wonder whist,
Smoothly the waters kissed,
Whispering new joys to the mild Ocean,
Who now hath quite forgot to rave,
While birds of calm sit brooding on the charmed wave.

VI

The stars, with deep amaze,
Stand fixed in steadfast gaze,
Bending one way their precious influence,
And will not take their flight,
For all the morning light,
Or Lucifer that often warned them thence;
But in their glimmering orbs did glow,
Until their Lord himself bespake, and bid them go.

VII

And, though the shady gloom
Had given day her room,
The Sun himself withheld his wonted speed,
And hid his head of shame,
As his inferior flame
The new-enlightened world no more should need:
He saw a greater Sun appear
Than his bright Throne or burning axletree could bear.

VIII

The Shepherds on the lawn,
Or ere the point of dawn,
Sat simply chatting in a rustic row;
Full little thought they than
That the mighty Pan
Was kindly come to live with them below:
Perhaps their loves, or else their sheep,
Was all that did their silly thoughts so busy keep.

IX

When such music sweet

Their hearts and ears did greet
As never was by mortal finger strook,
Divinely-warbled voice
Answering the stringèd noise,
As all their souls in blissful rapture took:
The air, such pleasure loth to lose,
With thousand echoes still prolongs each heavenly close.

X

Nature, that heard such sound
Beneath the hollow round
Of Cynthia's seat the airy Region thrilling,
Now was almost won
To think her part was done,
And that her reign had here its last fulfilling:
She knew such harmony alone
Could hold all Heaven and Earth in happier union.

XI

At last surrounds their sight
A globe of circular light,
That with long beams the shamefaced Night arrayed;
The helmèd Cherubim
And sworded Seraphim
Are seen in glittering ranks with wings displayed,
Harping in loud and solemn quire,
With unexpressive notes, to Heaven's newborn Heir.

XII

Such music (as 'tis said)
Before was never made,
But when of old the Sons of Morning sung,
While the Creator great
His constellations set,
And the well-balanced World on hinges hung,
And cast the dark foundations deep,
And bid the weltering waves their oozy channel keep.

XIII

Ring out, ye crystal spheres!
Once bless our human ears,
If ye have power to touch our senses so;
And let your silver chime
Move in melodious time;
And let the bass of heaven's deep organ blow;
And with your ninefold harmony
Make up full consort of the angelic symphony.

XIV

For, if such holy song
Enwrap our fancy long,
Time will run back and fetch the Age of Gold;

And speckled Vanity
Will sicken soon and die,
And leprous Sin will melt from earthly mould;
And Hell itself will pass away,
And leave her dolorous mansions of the peering day.

XV
Yes, Truth and Justice then
Will down return to men,
The enamelled arras of the rainbow wearing;
And Mercy set between,
Throned in celestial sheen,
With radiant feet the tissued clouds down steering;
And Heaven, as at some festival,
Will open wide the gates of her high palace-hall.

XVI
But wisest Fate says No,
This must not yet be so;
The Babe lies yet in smiling infancy
That on the bitter cross
Must redeem our loss,
So both himself and us to glorify:
Yet first, to those chained in sleep,
The wakeful trump of doom must thunder through the deep,

XVII
With such a horrid clang
As on Mount Sinai rang,
While the red fire and smouldering clouds outbrake:
The aged Earth, aghast
With terror of that blast,
Shall from the surface to the centre shake,
When, at the world's last sessiön,
The dreadful Judge in middle air shall spread his throne.

XVIII
And then at last our bliss
Full and perfect is,
But now begins; for from this happy day
The Old Dragon under ground,
In straiter limits bound,
Not half so far casts his usurpèd sway,
And, wroth to see his Kingdom fail,
Swindges the scaly horror of his folded tail.

XIX
The Oracles are dumb;
No voice or hideous hum
Runs through the archèd roof in words deceiving.
Apollo from his shrine
Can no more divine,

Will hollow shriek the steep of Delphos leaving.
No nightly trance, or breathèd spell,
Inspires the pale-eyed Priest from the prophetic cell.

XX
The lonely mountains o'er,
And the resounding shore,
A voice of weeping heard and loud lament;
Edgèd with poplar pale,
From haunted spring, and dale
The parting Genius is with sighing sent;
With flower-inwoven tresses torn
The Nymphs in twilight shade of tangled thickets mourn.

XXI
In consecrated earth,
And on the holy hearth,
The Lars and Lemures moan with midnight plaint;
In urns, and altars round,
A drear and dying sound
Affrights the Flamens at their service quaint;
And the chill marble seems to sweat,
While each peculiar power forgoes his wonted seat.

XXII
Peor and Baälim
Forsake their temples dim,
With that twice-battered god of Palestine;
And moonèd Ashtaroth,
Heaven's Queen and Mother both,
Now sits not girt with tapers' holy shine:
The Libyc Hammon shrinks his horn;
In vain the Tyrian maids their wounded Thammuz mourn.

XXIII
And sullen Moloch, fled,
Hath left in shadows dread
His burning idol all of blackest hue;
In vain with cymbals' ring
They call the grisly king,
In dismal dance about the furnace blue;
The brutish gods of Nile as fast,
Isis, and Orus, and the dog Anubis, haste.

XXIV
Nor is Osiris seen
In Memphian grove or green,
Trampling the unshowered grass with lowings loud;
Nor can he be at rest
Within his sacred chest;
Nought but profoundest Hell can be his shroud;
In vain, with timbreled anthems dark,

The sable-stolèd Sorcerers bear his worshiped ark.

XXV

He feels from Juda's land
The dreaded Infant's hand;
The rays of Bethlehem blind his dusky eyn;
Nor all the gods beside
Longer dare abide,
Not Typhon huge ending in snaky twine:
Our Babe, to show his Godhead true,
Can in his swaddling bands control the damnèd crew.

XXVI

So, when the Sun in bed,
Curtained with cloudy red,
Pillows his chin upon an orient wave,
The flocking shadows pale
Troop to the infernal jail,
Each fettered ghost slips to his several grave,
And the yellow-skirted Fays
Fly after the night-steeds, leaving their moon-loved maze.

XXVII

But see! the Virgin blest
Hath laid her Babe to rest,
Time is our tedious song should here have ending:
Heaven's youngest-teemèd star
Hath fixed her polished car,
Her sleeping Lord with handmaid lamp attending;
And all about the courtly stable
Bright-harnessed Angels sit in order serviceable.

To His Coy Mistress by Andrew Marvell
Had we but world enough, and time,
This coyness, lady, were no crime.
We would sit down and think which way
To walk, and pass our long love's day;
Thou by the Indian Ganges' side
Shouldst rubies find; I by the tide
Of Humber would complain. I would
Love you ten years before the Flood;
And you should, if you please, refuse
Till the conversion of the Jews.
My vegetable love should grow
Vaster than empires, and more slow.
An hundred years should go to praise
Thine eyes, and on thy forehead gaze;
Two hundred to adore each breast,
But thirty thousand to the rest;
An age at least to every part,
And the last age should show your heart.

For, lady, you deserve this state,
Nor would I love at lower rate.

But at my back I always hear
Time's winged chariot hurrying near;
And yonder all before us lie
Deserts of vast eternity.
Thy beauty shall no more be found,
Nor, in thy marble vault, shall sound
My echoing song; then worms shall try
That long preserv'd virginity,
And your quaint honour turn to dust,
And into ashes all my lust.
The grave's a fine and private place,
But none I think do there embrace.

Now therefore, while the youthful hue
Sits on thy skin like morning dew,
And while thy willing soul transpires
At every pore with instant fires,
Now let us sport us while we may;
And now, like am'rous birds of prey,
Rather at once our time devour,
Than languish in his slow-chapp'd power.
Let us roll all our strength, and all
Our sweetness, up into one ball;
And tear our pleasures with rough strife
Thorough the iron gates of life.
Thus, though we cannot make our sun
Stand still, yet we will make him run.

A True Born Englishman by Daniel Defoe
Thus from a mixture of all kinds began,
That het'rogeneous thing, an Englishman:
In eager rapes, and furious lust begot,
Betwixt a painted Britain and a Scot.
Whose gend'ring off-spring quickly learn'd to bow,
And yoke their heifers to the Roman plough:
From whence a mongrel half-bred race there came,
With neither name, nor nation, speech nor fame.
In whose hot veins new mixtures quickly ran,
Infus'd betwixt a Saxon and a Dane.
While their rank daughters, to their parents just,
Receiv'd all nations with promiscuous lust.
This nauseous brood directly did contain
The well-extracted blood of Englishmen.

Which medly canton'd in a heptarchy,
A rhapsody of nations to supply,
Among themselves maintain'd eternal wars,
And still the ladies lov'd the conquerors.

The western Angles all the rest subdu'd;
A bloody nation, barbarous and rude:
Who by the tenure of the sword possest
One part of Britain, and subdu'd the rest
And as great things denominate the small,
The conqu'ring part gave title to the whole.
The Scot, Pict, Britain, Roman, Dane, submit,
And with the English-Saxon all unite:
And these the mixture have so close pursu'd,
The very name and memory's subdu'd:
No Roman now, no Britain does remain;
Wales strove to separate, but strove in vain:
The silent nations undistinguish'd fall,
And Englishman's the common name for all.
Fate jumbled them together, God knows how;
What e'er they were they're true-born English now.

The wonder which remains is at our pride,
To value that which all wise men deride.
For Englishmen to boast of generation,
Cancels their knowledge, and lampoons the nation.
A true-born Englishman's a contradiction,
In speech an irony, in fact a fiction.
A banter made to be a test of fools,
Which those that use it justly ridicules.
A metaphor invented to express
A man a-kin to all the universe.

For as the Scots, as learned men ha' said,
Throughout the world their wand'ring seed ha' spread;
So open-handed England, 'tis believ'd,
Has all the gleanings of the world receiv'd.

Some think of England 'twas our Saviour meant,
The Gospel should to all the world be sent:
Since, when the blessed sound did hither reach,
They to all nations might be said to preach.

'Tis well that virtue gives nobility,
How shall we else the want of birth and blood supply?
Since scarce one family is left alive,
Which does not from some foreigner derive.

A Song For St Cecilia's Day by John Dryden
1
From harmony, from heavenly harmony
This universal frame began.
When Nature underneath a heap
Of jarring atoms lay,
And could not heave her head,

The tuneful voice was heard from high:
"Arise, ye more than dead!"
Then cold and hot and moist and dry
In order to their stations leap,
And Music's power obey.
From harmony, from heavenly harmony
This universal frame began;
From harmony to harmony
Through all the compass of the notes it ran,
The diapason closing full in Man.

2

What passion cannot Music raise and quell?
When Jubal struck the corded shell,
His list'ning brethren stood around,
And, wond'ring, on their faces fell
To worship that celestial sound,
Less than a god they thought there could not dwell
Within the hollow of that shell
That spoke so sweetly and so well.
What passion cannot Music raise and quell?

3

The trumpet's loud clangor
Excites us to arms,
With shrill notes of anger
And mortal alarms.
The double double double beat
Of the thundering drum
Cries, "Hark, the foes come!
Charge, charge, 't is too late to retreat!"

4

The soft complaining flute
In dying notes discovers
The woes of hopeless lovers,
Whose dirge is whispered by the warbling lute.

5

Sharp violins proclaim
Their jealous pangs and desperation,
Fury, frantic indignation,
Depth of pains and height of passion,
For the fair disdainful dame.

6

But oh! what art can teach,
What human voice can reach
The sacred organ's praise?
Notes inspiring holy love,
Notes that wing their heavenly ways
To mend the choirs above.

7
Orpheus could lead the savage race,
And trees unrooted left their place,
Sequacious of the lyre;
But bright Cecilia raised the wonder higher:
When to her organ vocal breath was given,
An angel heard, and straight appeared
Mistaking earth for heaven.

GRAND CHORUS
As from the power of sacred lays
The spheres began to move,
And sung the great Creator's praise
To all the blest above:
So, when the last and dreadful hour
This crumbling pageant shall devour,
The trumpet shall be heard on high,
The dead shall live, the living die,
And Music shall untune the sky.

The Rape Of The Lock by Alexander Pope
Part 1
What dire Offence from am'rous Causes springs,
What mighty Contests rise from trivial Things,
I sing This Verse to C---, Muse! is due;
This, ev'n *Belinda* may vouchfafe to view:
Slight is the Subject, but not so the Praise,
If She inspire, and He approve my Lays.
Say what strange Motive, Goddess! cou'd compel
A well-bred *Lord* t'assault a gentle *Belle?*
Oh say what stranger Cause, yet unexplor'd,
Cou'd make a gentle *Belle* reject a *Lord*?
And dwells such Rage in softest Bosoms then?
And lodge such daring Souls in Little Men?
Sol thro' white Curtains shot a tim'rous Ray,
And op'd those Eyes that must eclipse the Day;
Now Lapdogs give themselves the rowzing Shake,
And sleepless Lovers, just at Twelve, awake:
Thrice rung the Bell, the Slipper knock'd the Ground,
And the press'd Watch return'd a silver Sound.
Belinda still her downy Pillow prest,
Her Guardian *Sylph* prolong'd the balmy Rest.
'Twas he had summon'd to her silent Bed
The Morning-Dream that hover'd o'er her Head.
A Youth more glitt'ring than a *Birth-night Beau*,
(That ev'n in Slumber caus'd her Cheek to glow)
Seem'd to her Ear his winning Lips to lay,
And thus in Whispers said, or seem'd to say.
Fairest of Mortals, thou distinguish'd Care
Of thousand bright Inhabitants of Air!

If e'er one Vision touch'd thy infant Thought,
Of all the Nurse and all the Priest have taught,
Of airy Elves by Moonlight Shadows seen,
The silver Token, and the circled Green,
Or Virgins visited by Angel-Pow'rs,
With Golden Crowns and Wreaths of heav'nly Flowers,
Hear and believe! thy own Importance know,
Nor bound thy narrow Views to Things below.
Some secret Truths from Learned Pride conceal'd,
To Maids alone and Children are reveal'd:
What tho' no Credit doubting Wits may give?
The Fair and Innocent shall still believe.
Know then, unnumbered Spirits round thee fly,
The light *Militia* of the lower Sky;
These, tho' unseen, are ever on the Wing,
Hang o'er the *Box*, and hover round the *Ring*.
Think what an Equipage thou hast in Air,
And view with scorn *Two Pages* and a *Chair*.
As now your own, our Beings were of old,
And once inclos'd in Woman's beauteous Mold;
Thence, by a soft Transition, we repair
From earthly Vehicles to these of Air.
Think not, when Woman's transient Breath is fled,
That all her Vanities at once are dead:
Succeeding Vanities she still regards,
And tho' she plays no more, o'erlooks the Cards.
Her Joy in gilded Chariots, when alive,
And Love of *Ombre*, after Death survive.
For when the Fair in all their Pride expire,
To their first Elements the Souls retire:
The Sprights of fiery Termagants in Flame
Mount up, and take a *Salamander*'s Name.
Soft yielding Minds to Water glide away,
And sip with *Nymphs*, their Elemental Tea.
The graver Prude sinks downward to a *Gnome*,
In search of Mischief still on Earth to roam.
The light Coquettes in *Sylphs* aloft repair,
And sport and flutter in the Fields of Air.
Know farther yet; Whoever fair and chaste
Rejects Mankind, is by some *Sylph* embrac'd:
For Spirits, freed from mortal Laws, with ease
Assume what Sexes and what Shapes they please.
What guards the Purity of melting Maids,
In Courtly Balls, and Midnight Masquerades,
Safe from the treach'rous Friend, and daring Spark,
The Glance by Day, the Whisper in the Dark;
When kind Occasion prompts their warm Desires,
When Musick softens, and when Dancing fires?
'Tis but their *Sylph*, the wise Celestials know,
Tho' *Honour* is the Word with Men below.
Some Nymphs there are, too conscious of their Face,
For Life predestin'd to the *Gnomes* Embrace.

These swell their Prospects and exalt their Pride,
When Offers are disdain'd, and Love deny'd.
Then gay Ideas crowd the vacant Brain;
While Peers and Dukes, and all their sweeping Train,
And Garters, Stars, and Coronets appear,
And in soft Sounds, *Your Grace* salutes their Ear.
'Tis these that early taint the Female Soul,
Instruct the Eyes of young *Coquettes* to roll,
Teach Infants Cheeks a bidden Blush to know,
And little Hearts to flutter at a *Beau*.
Oft when the World imagine Women stray,
The *Sylphs* thro' mystick Mazes guide thier Way,
Thro' all the giddy Circle they pursue,
And old Impertinence expel by new.
What tender Maid but must a Victim fall
To one Man's Treat, but for another's Ball?
When *Florio* speaks, what Virgin could withstand,
If gentle *Damon* did not squeeze her Hand?
With varying Vanities, from ev'ry Part,
They shift the moving Toyshop of their Heart;
Where Wigs with Wigs, with Sword-knots Sword-knots strive,
Beaus banish Beaus, and Coaches Coaches drive.
This erring Mortals Levity may call,
Oh blind to Truth! the *Sylphs* contrive it all.
Of these am I, who thy Protection claim,
A watchful Sprite, and *Ariel* is my Name.
Late, as I rang'd the Crystal Wilds of Air,
In the clear Mirror of thy ruling *Star*
I saw, alas! some dread Event impend,
E're to the Main this Morning Sun descend.
But Heav'n reveals not what, or how, or where:
Warn'd by thy *Sylph*, oh Pious Maid beware!
This to disclose is all thy Guardian can.
Beware of all, but most beware of Man!
He said; when *Shock*, who thought she slept too long,
Leapt up, and wak'd his Mistress with his Tongue.
'Twas then *Belinda*, if Report say true,
Thy Eyes first open'd on a *Billet-doux*.
Wounds, *Charms*, and *Ardors*, were no sooner read,
But all the Vision vanish'd from thy Head.
And now, unveil'd, the *Toilet* stands display'd,
Each Silver Vase in mystic Order laid.
First, rob'd in White, the Nymph intent adores
With Head uncover'd, the *cosmetic* Pow'rs.
A heav'nly Image in the Glass appears,
To that she bends, to that her Eyes she rears;
Th' inferior Priestess, at her Altar's side,
Trembling, begins the sacred Rites of Pride.
Unnumber'd Treasures ope at once, and here
The various Off'rings of the World appear;
From each she nicely culls with curious Toil,
And decks the Goddess with the glitt'ring Spoil.

This Casket *India*'s glowing Gems unlocks,
And all *Arabia* breathes from yonder Box.
The Tortoise here and Elephant unite,
Transform'd to *Combs*, the speckled and the white.
Here Files of Pins extend their shining Rows,
Puffs, Powders, Patches, Bibles, Billet-doux.
Now awful Beauty puts on all its Arms;
The Fair each moment rises in her Charms,
Repairs her Smiles, awakens ev'ry Grace,
And calls forth all the Wonders of her Face;
Sees by Degrees a purer Blush arise,
And keener Lightnings quicken in her Eyes.
The busy *Sylphs* surround their darling Care;
These set the Head, and those divide the Hair,
Some fold the Sleeve, while others plait the Gown;
And *Betty*'s prais'd for Labours not her own.

Part 2
Not with more Glories, in th' Etherial Plain,
The Sun first rises o'er the purpled Main,
Than issuing forth, the Rival of his Beams
Lanch'd on the Bosom of the Silver *Thames*.
Fair Nymphs, and well-drest Youths around her shone,
But ev'ry Eye was fix'd on her alone.
On her white Breast a sparkling *Cross* she wore,
Which *Jews* might kiss, and Infidels adore.
Her lively Looks a sprightly Mind disclose,
Quick as her Eyes, and as unfix'd as those:
Favours to none, to all she Smiles extends,
Oft she rejects, but never once offends.
Bright as the Sun, her Eyes the Gazers strike,
And, like the sun, they shine on all alike.
Yet graceful Ease, and Sweetness void of Pride,
Might hide her Faults, if *Belles* had faults to hide:
If to her share some Female Errors fall,
Look on her Face, and you'll forget 'em all.
This Nymph, to the Destruction of Mankind,
Nourish'd two Locks, which graceful hung behind
In equal Curls, and well conspir'd to deck
With shining Ringlets her smooth Iv'ry Neck.
Love in these Labyrinths his Slaves detains,
And mighty Hearts are held in slender Chains.
With hairy Sprindges we the Birds betray,
Slight Lines of Hair surprize the Finny Prey,
Fair Tresses Man's Imperial Race insnare,
And Beauty draws us with a single Hair.
Th' Adventrous *Baron* the bright Locks admir'd,
He saw, he wish'd, and to the Prize aspir'd:
Resolv'd to win, he meditates the way,
By Force to ravish, or by Fraud betray;
For when Success a Lover's Toil attends,
Few ask, if Fraud or Force attain'd his Ends.

For this, e're *Phoebus* rose, he had implor'd
Propitious Heav'n, and ev'ry Pow'r ador'd,
But chiefly *Love*--to *Love* an Altar built,
Of twelve vast *French* Romances, neatly gilt.
There lay three Garters, half a Pair of Gloves;
And all the Trophies of his former Loves.
With tender *Billet-doux* he lights the Pyre,
And breathes three am'rous Sighs to raise the Fire.
Then prostrate falls, and begs with ardent Eyes
Soon to obtain, and long possess the Prize:
The Pow'rs gave Ear, and granted half his Pray'r,
The rest, the Winds dispers'd in empty Air.
But now secure the painted Vessel glides,
The Sun-beams trembling on the floating Tydes,
While melting Musick steals upon the Sky,
And soften'd Sounds along the Waters die.
Smooth flow the Waves, the Zephyrs gently play
Belinda smil'd, and all the World was gay.
All but the *Sylph* With careful Thoughts opprest,
Th' impending Woe sate heavy on his Breast.
He summons strait his Denizens of Air;
The lucid Squadrons round the Sails repair:
Soft o'er the Shrouds Aerial Whispers breathe,
That seem'd but *Zephyrs* to the Train beneath.
Some to the Sun their Insect-Wings unfold,
Waft on the Breeze, or sink in Clouds of Gold.
Transparent Forms, too fine for mortal Sight,
Their fluid Bodies half dissolv'd in Light.
Loose to the Wind their airy Garments flew,
Thin glitt'ring Textures of the filmy Dew;
Dipt in the richest Tincture of the Skies,
Where Light disports in ever-mingling Dies,
While ev'ry Beam new transient Colours flings,
Colours that change whene'er they wave their Wings.
Amid the Circle, on the gilded Mast,
Superior by the Head, was *Ariel* plac'd;
His Purple Pinions opening to the Sun,
He rais'd his Azure Wand, and thus begun.
Ye *Sylphs* and *Sylphids*, to your Chief give Ear,
Fays, Fairies, Genii, Elves, and *Daemons* hear!
Ye know the Spheres and various Tasks assign'd,
By Laws Eternal, to th' Aerial Kind.
Some in the Fields of purest *AEther* play,
And bask and whiten in the Blaze of Day.
Some guide the Course of wandring Orbs on high,
Or roll the Planets thro' the boundless Sky.
Some less refin'd, beneath the Moon's pale Light
Hover, and catch the shooting stars by Night;
Or suck the Mists in grosser Air below,
Or dip their Pinions in the painted Bow,
Or brew fierce Tempests on the wintry Main,
Or o'er the Glebe distill the kindly Rain.

Others on Earth o'er human Race preside,
Watch all their Ways, and all their Actions guide:
Of these the Chief the Care of Nations own,
And guard with Arms Divine the *British Throne*.
Our humbler Province is to tend the Fair,
Not a less pleasing, tho' less glorious Care.
To save the Powder from too rude a Gale,
Nor let th' imprison'd Essences exhale,
To draw fresh Colours from the vernal Flow'rs,
To steal from Rainbows ere they drop in Show'rs
A brighter Wash; to curl their waving Hairs,
Assist their Blushes, and inspire their Airs;
Nay oft, in Dreams, Invention we bestow,
To change a *Flounce*, or add a *Furbelo*.
This Day, black Omens threat the brightest Fair
That e'er deserv'd a watchful Spirit's Care;
Some dire Disaster, or by Force, or Slight,
But what, or where, the Fates have wrapt in Night.
Whether the Nymph shall break *Diana*'s Law,
Or some frail *China* Jar receive a Flaw,
Or stain her Honour, or her new Brocade,
Forget her Pray'rs, or miss a Masquerade,
Or lose her Heart, or Necklace, at a Ball;
Or whether Heav'n has doom'd that *Shock* must fall.
Haste then ye Spirits! to your Charge repair;
The flutt'ring Fan be *Zephyretta*'s Care;
The Drops to thee, *Brillante*, we consign;
And *Momentilla*, let the Watch be thine;
Do thou, *Crispissa*, tend her fav'rite Lock;
Ariel himself shall be the Guard of *Shock*.
To Fifty chosen *Sylphs*, of special Note,
We trust th' important Charge, the *Petticoat*.
Oft have we known that sev'nfold Fence to fail;
Tho' stiff with Hoops, and arm'd with Ribs of Whale.
Form a strong Line about the Silver Bound,
And guard the wide Circumference around.
Whatever spirit, careless of his Charge,
His Post neglects, or leaves the Fair at large,
Shall feel sharp Vengeance soon o'ertake his Sins,
Be stopt in *Vials*, or transfixt with *Pins*.
Or plung'd in Lakes of bitter *Washes* lie,
Or wedg'd whole Ages in a *Bodkin's* Eye:
Gums and *Pomatums* shall his Flight restrain,
While clog'd he beats his silken Wings in vain;
Or Alom-*Stypticks* with contracting Power
Shrink his thin Essence like a rivell'd Flower.
Or as *Ixion* fix'd, the Wretch shall feel
The giddy Motion of the whirling Mill,
In Fumes of burning Chocolate shall glow,
And tremble at the Sea that froaths below!
He spoke; the Spirits from the Sails descend;
Some, Orb in Orb, around the Nymph extend,

Some thrid the mazy Ringlets of her Hair,
Some hang upon the Pendants of her Ear;
With beating Hearts the dire Event they wait,
Anxious, and trembling for the Birth of Fate.

Part 3
Close by those Meads for ever crown'd with Flow'rs,
Where *Thames* with Pride surveys his rising Tow'rs,
There stands a Structure of Majestick Frame,
Which from the neighb'ring *Hampton* takes its Name.
Here *Britain*'s Statesmen oft the Fall foredoom
Of Foreign Tyrants, and of Nymphs at home;
Here Thou, great *Anna*! whom three Realms obey,
Dost sometimes Counsel take and sometimes *Tea*.
Hither the Heroes and the Nymphs resort,
To taste awhile the Pleasures of a Court;
In various Talk th' instructive hours they past,
Who gave the *Ball*, or paid the *Visit* last:
One speaks the Glory of the *British Queen*,
And one describes a charming *Indian Screen*.
A third interprets Motions, Looks, and Eyes;
At ev'ry Word a Reputation dies.
Snuff, or the *Fan*, supply each Pause of Chat,
With singing, laughing, ogling, and all that.
Mean while declining from the Noon of Day,
The Sun obliquely shoots his burning Ray;
The hungry Judges soon the Sentence sign,
And Wretches hang that Jury-men may Dine;
The Merchant from th'*exchange* returns in Peace,
And the long Labours of the *Toilette* cease
Belinda now, whom Thirst of Fame invites,
Burns to encounter two adventrous Knights,
At *Ombre* singly to decide their Doom;
And swells her Breast with Conquests yet to come.
Strait the three Bands prepare in Arms to join,
Each Band the number of the Sacred Nine.
Soon as she spreads her Hand, th' Aerial Guard
Descend, and sit on each important Card,
First *Ariel* perch'd upon a *Matadore*,
Then each, according to the Rank they bore;
For *Sylphs*, yet mindful of their ancient Race,
Are, as when Women, wondrous fond of place.
Behold, four *Kings* in Majesty rever'd,
With hoary Whiskers and a forky Beard;
And four fair *Queens* whose hands sustain a Flow'r,
Th' expressive Emblem of their softer Pow'r;
Four *Knaves* in Garbs succinct, a trusty Band,
Caps on their heads, and Halberds in their hand;
And Particolour'd Troops, a shining Train,
Draw forth to Combat on the Velvet Plain.
The skilful Nymph reviews her Force with Care;
Let Spades be Trumps, she said, and Trumps they were.

Now move to War her Sable *Matadores*,
In Show like Leaders of the swarthy *Moors*.
Spadillio first, unconquerable Lord!
Led off two captive Trumps, and swept the Board.
As many more *Manillio* forc'd to yield,
And march'd a Victor from the verdant Field.
Him *Basto* follow'd, but his Fate more hard
Gain'd but one Trump and one *Plebeian* Card.
With his broad Sabre next, a Chief in Years,
The hoary Majesty of *Spades* appears;
Puts forth one manly Leg, to sight reveal'd;
The rest his many-colour'd Robe conceal'd.
The Rebel-Knave, who dares his Prince engage,
Proves the just Victim of his Royal Rage.
Ev'n mighty *Pam* that Kings and Queens o'erthrow,
And mow'd down Armies in the Fights of *Lu*,
Sad Chance of War! now, destitute of Aid,
Falls undistinguish'd by the Victor *Spade*.
Thus far both Armies to *Belinda* yield;
Now to the *Baron* Fate inclines the Field.
His warlike *Amazon* her Host invades,
Th' Imperial Consort of the Crown of *Spades*.
The *Club's* black Tyrant first her Victim dy'd,
Spite of his haughty Mien, and barb'rous Pride:
What boots the Regal Circle on his Head,
His Giant Limbs in State unwieldy spread?
That long behind he trails his pompous Robe,
And of all Monarchs only grasps the Globe?
The *Baron* now his *Diamonds* pours apace;
Th' embroider'd *King* who shows but half his Face,
And his refulgent *Queen*, with Pow'rs combin'd,
Of broken Troops an easie Conquest find.
Clubs, Diamonds, Hearts, in wild Disorder seen,
With Throngs promiscuous strow the level Green.
Thus when dispers'd a routed Army runs,
Of *Asia*'s Troops, and *Africk*'s Sable Sons,
With like Confusion different Nations fly,
In various habits and of various Dye,
The pierc'd Battalions dis-united fall,
In Heaps on Heaps; one Fate o'erwhelms them all.
The *Knave* of *Diamonds* now tries his wily Arts,
And wins (oh shameful Chance!) the *Queen* of *Hearts*.
At this, the Blood the Virgin's Cheek forsook,
A livid Paleness spreads o'er all her Look;
She sees, and trembles at th' approaching Ill,
Just in the Jaws of Ruin, and *Codille*.
And now, (as oft in some distemper'd State)
On one nice *Trick* depends the gen'ral Fate.
An *Ace* of Hearts steps forth: The *King* unseen
Lurk'd in her Hand, and mourn'd his captive *Queen*.
He springs to Vengeance with an eager pace,
And falls like Thunder on the prostrate *Ace*.

The Nymph exulting fills with Shouts the Sky,
The Walls, the Woods, and long Canals reply.
Oh thoughtless Mortals! ever blind to Fate,
Too soon dejected, and too soon elate!
Sudden these Honours shall be snatch'd away,
And curs'd for ever this Victorious Day.
For lo! the Board with Cups and Spoons is crown'd,
The Berries crackle, and the Mill turns round.
On shining Altars of *Japan* they raise
The silver Lamp; the fiery Spirits blaze.
From silver Spouts the grateful Liquors glide,
And *China*'s Earth receives the smoking Tyde.
At once they gratify their Scent and Taste,
While frequent Cups prolong the rich Repast.
Strait hover round the Fair her Airy Band;
Some, as she sip'd, the fuming Liquor fann'd,
Some o'er her Lap their careful Plumes display'd,
Trembling, and conscious of the rich Brocade.
Coffee, (which makes the Politician wise,
And see thro' all things with his half shut Eyes)
Sent up in Vapours to the *Baron*'s Brain
New Stratagems, the radiant Lock to gain.
Ah cease rash Youth! desist e'er 'tis too late,
Fear the just Gods, and think of *Scylla*'s Fate!
Chang'd to a Bird, and sent to flit in Air,
She dearly pays for *Nisus'* injur'd Hair!
But when to Mischief Mortals bend their Will,
How soon they find fit Instruments of Ill!
Just then, *Clarissa* drew with tempting Grace
A two-edg'd Weapon from her shining Case;
So Ladies in Romance assist their Knight,
Present the Spear, and arm him for the Fight.
He takes the Gift with rev'rence, and extends
The little Engine on his Finger's Ends:
This just behind *Belinda*'s Neck he spread,
As o'er the fragrant Steams she bends her Head:
Swift to the Lock a thousand Sprights repair,
A thousand Wings, by turns, blow back the Hair,
And thrice they twitch'd the Diamond in her Ear,
Thrice she look'd back, and thrice the Foe drew near.
Just in that instant, anxious *Ariel* sought
The close Recesses of the Virgin's Thought;
As on the Nosegay in her Breast reclin'd,
He watch'd th' Ideas rising in her Mind,
Sudden he view'd, in spite of all her Art,
An Earthly Lover lurking at her Heart.
Amaz'd, confus'd, he found his Pow'r expir'd,
Resign'd to Fate, and with a Sigh retir'd.
The Peer now spreads the glitt'ring *Forfex* wide,
T'inclose the Lock; now joins it, to divide.
Ev'n then, before the fatal Engine clos'd,
A wretched *Sylph* too fondly interpos'd;

Fate urg'd the Sheers, and cut the *Sylph* in twain,
(But Airy Substance soon unites again)
The meeting Points that sacred Hair dissever
From the fair Head, for ever and for ever!
Then flash'd the living Lightnings from her Eyes,
And Screams of Horror rend th' affrighted Skies.
Not louder Shrieks to pitying Heav'n are cast,
When Husbands or when Lap-dogs breath their last,
Or when rich *China* Vessels, fal'n from high,
In glittring Dust and painted Fragments lie!
Let Wreaths of Triumph now my Temples twine,
(The Victor cry'd) the glorious Prize is mine!
While Fish in Streams, or Birds delight in Air,
Or in a Coach and Six the *British* Fair,
As long as *Atalantis* shall be read,
Or the small Pillow grace a Lady's Bed,
While *Visits* shall be paid on solemn Days,
When numerous Wax-lights in bright Order blaze,
While Nymphs take Treats, or Assignations give,
So long my Honour, Name, and Praise shall live!
What Time wou'd spare, from Steel receives its date,
And Monuments, like Men, submit to Fate!
Steel cou'd the Labour of the Gods destroy,
And strike to Dust th' Imperial Tow'rs of *Troy*.
Steel cou'd the Works of mortal Pride confound,
And hew Triumphal Arches to the Ground.
What Wonder then, fair Nymph! thy Hairs shou'd feel
The conqu'ring Force of unresisted Steel?

Part 4
But anxious Cares the pensive Nymph opprest,
And secret Passions labour'd in her Breast.
Not youthful Kings in Battel seiz'd alive,
Not scornful Virgins who their Charms survive,
Not ardent Lovers robb'd of all their Bliss,
Not ancient Ladies when refus'd a Kiss,
Not Tyrants fierce that unrepenting die,
Not *Cynthia* when her *Manteau*'s pinn'd awry,
E'er felt such Rage, Resentment and Despair,
As Thou, sad Virgin! for thy ravish'd Hair.
For, that sad moment, when the *Sylphs* withdrew,
And *Ariel* weeping from *Belinda* flew,
Umbriel, a dusky melancholy Spright,
As ever sully'd the fair face of Light,
Down to the Central Earth, his proper Scene,
Repairs to search the gloomy Cave of *Spleen*.
Swift on his sooty Pinions flitts the *Gnome*,
And in a Vapour reach'd the dismal Dome.
No cheerful Breeze this sullen Region knows,
The dreaded *East* is all the Wind that blows.
Here, in a Grotto, sheltred close from Air,
And screen'd in Shades from Day's detested Glare,

She sighs for ever on her pensive Bed,
Pain at her side, and *Megrim* at her Head.
Two Handmaids wait the Throne: Alike in Place,
But diff'ring far in Figure and in Face.
Here stood *Ill-nature* like an *ancient Maid*,
Her wrinkled Form in *Black* and *White* array'd;
With store of Pray'rs, for Mornings, Nights, and Noons,
Her Hand is fill'd; her Bosom with Lampoons.
There *Affectation* with a sickly Mien
Shows in her Cheek the Roses of Eighteen,
Practis'd to Lisp, and hang the Head aside,
Faints into Airs, and languishes with Pride;
On the rich Quilt sinks with becoming Woe,
Wrapt in a Gown, for Sickness, and for Show.
The Fair ones feel such Maladies as these,
When each new Night-Dress gives a new Disease.
A constant *Vapour* o'er the Palace flies;
Strange Phantoms rising as the Mists arise;
Dreadful, as Hermit's Dreams in haunted Shades,
Or bright as Visions of expiring Maids.
Now glaring Fiends, and Snakes on rolling Spires,
Pale Spectres, gaping Tombs, and Purple Fires:
Now Lakes of liquid Gold, *Elysian* Scenes,
And Crystal Domes, and Angels in Machines.
Unnumber'd Throngs on ev'ry side are seen
Of Bodies chang'd to various Forms by *Spleen*.
Here living *Teapots* stand, one Arm held out,
One bent; the Handle this, and that the Spout:
A Pipkin there like *Homer's Tripod* walks;
Here sighs a Jar, and there a Goose Pie talks;
Men prove with Child, as pow'rful Fancy works,
And Maids turn'd Bottels, call aloud for Corks.
Safe past the *Gnome* thro' this fantastick Band,
A Branch of healing *Spleenwort* in his hand.
Then thus addrest the Pow'r--Hail wayward Queen!
Who rule the Sex to Fifty from Fifteen,
Parent of Vapors and of Female Wit,
Who give th' *Hysteric* or *Poetic* Fit,
On various Tempers act by various ways,
Make some take Physick, others scribble Plays;
Who cause the Proud their Visits to delay,
And send the Godly in a Pett, to pray.
A Nymph there is, that all thy Pow'r disdains,
And thousands more in equal Mirth maintains.
But oh! if e'er thy *Gnome* could spoil a Grace,
Or raise a Pimple on a beauteous Face,
Like Citron-Waters Matron's Cheeks inflame,
Or change Complexions at a losing Game;
If e'er with airy Horns I planted Heads,
Or rumpled Petticoats, or tumbled Beds,
Or caus'd Suspicion when no Soul was rude,
Or discompos'd the Head-dress of a Prude,

Or e'er to costive Lap-Dog gave Disease,
Which not the Tears of brightest Eyes could ease:
Hear me, and touch *Belinda* with Chagrin;
That single Act gives half the World the Spleen.
The Goddess with a discontented Air
Seems to reject him, tho' she grants his Pray'r.
A wondrous Bag with both her Hands she binds,
Like that where once *Ulysses* held the Winds;
There she collects the Force of Female Lungs,
Sighs, Sobs, and Passions, and the War of Tongues.
A Vial next she fills with fainting Fears,
Soft Sorrows, melting Griefs, and flowing Tears.
The *Gnome* rejoicing bears her Gift away,
Spreads his black Wings, and slowly mounts to Day.
Sunk in *Thalestris'* Arms the Nymph he found,
Her Eyes dejected and her Hair unbound.
Full o'er their Heads the swelling Bag he rent,
And all the Furies issued at the Vent.
Belinda burns with more than mortal Ire,
And fierce *Thalestris* fans the rising Fire.
O wretched Maid! she spread her hands, and cry'd,
(While *Hampton*'s Ecchos, wretched Maid reply'd)
Was it for this you took such constant Care
The *Bodkin, Comb*, and *Essence* to prepare;
For this your Locks in Paper-Durance bound,
For this with tort'ring Irons wreath'd around?
For this with Fillets strain'd your tender Head,
And bravely bore the double Loads of Lead?
Gods! shall the Ravisher display your Hair,
While the Fops envy, and the Ladies stare!
Honour forbid! at whose unrival'd Shrine
Ease, Pleasure, Virtue, All, our Sex resign.
Methinks already I your Tears survey,
Already hear the horrid things they say,
Already see you a degraded Toast,
And all your Honour in a Whisper lost!
How shall I, then, your helpless Fame defend?
'Twill then be Infamy to seem your Friend!
And shall this Prize, th' inestimable Prize,
Expos'd thro' Crystal to the gazing Eyes,
And heighten'd by the Diamond's circling Rays,
On that Rapacious Hand for ever blaze?
Sooner shall Grass in *Hide* Park *Circus* grow,
And Wits take Lodgings in the Sound of *Bow*;
Sooner let Earth, Air, Sea, to *Chaos* fall,
Men, Monkies, Lap-dogs, Parrots, perish all!
She said; then raging to *Sir Plume* repairs,
And bids her *Beau* demand the precious Hairs:
(*Sir Plume*, of *Amber Snuff-box* justly vain,
And the nice Conduct of a *clouded Cane*)
With earnest Eyes, and round unthinking Face,
He first the Snuff-box open'd, then the Case,

And thus broke out "My Lord, why, what the Devil?
"Z---ds! damn the Lock! 'fore Gad, you must be civil!
"Plague on't! 'tis past a Jest nay prithee, Pox!
"Give her the Hair he spoke, and rapp'd his Box.
It grieves me much (reply'd the Peer again)
Who speaks so well shou'd ever speak in vain.
But by this Lock, this sacred Lock I swear,
(Which never more shall join its parted Hair,
Which never more its Honours shall renew,
Clipt from the lovely Head where late it grew)
That while my Nostrils draw the vital Air,
This Hand, which won it, shall for ever wear.
He spoke, and speaking, in proud Triumph spread
The long-contended Honours of her Head.
But *Umbriel*, hateful *Gnome*! forbears not so;
He breaks the Vial whence the Sorrows flow.
Then see! the *Nymph* in beauteous Grief appears,
Her Eyes half languishing, half drown'd in Tears;
On her heav'd Bosom hung her drooping Head,
Which, with a Sigh, she rais'd; and thus she said.
For ever curs'd be this detested Day,
Which snatch'd my best, my fav'rite Curl away!
Happy! ah ten times happy, had I been,
If *Hampton-Court* these Eyes had never seen!
Yet am not I the first mistaken Maid,
By Love of *Courts* to num'rous Ills betray'd.
Oh had I rather un-admir'd remain'd
In some lone Isle, or distant *Northern* Land;
Where the gilt *Chariot* never marks the way,
Where none learn *Ombre*, none e'er taste *Bohea*!
There kept my Charms conceal'd from mortal Eye,
Like Roses that in Desarts bloom and die.
What mov'd my Mind with youthful Lords to rome?
O had I stay'd, and said my Pray'rs at home!
'Twas this, the Morning *Omens* seem'd to tell;
Thrice from my trembling hand the *Patch-box* fell;
The tott'ring *China* shook without a Wind,
Nay, *Poll* sate mute, and *Shock* was most Unkind!
A *Sylph* too warn'd me of the Threats of Fate,
In mystic Visions, now believ'd too late!
See the poor Remnants of these slighted Hairs!
My hands shall rend what ev'n thy Rapine spares:
These, in two sable Ringlets taught to break,
Once gave new Beauties to the snowie Neck.
The Sister-Lock now sits uncouth, alone,
And in its Fellow's Fate foresees its own;
Uncurl'd it hangs, the fatal Sheers demands;
And tempts once more thy sacrilegious Hands.
Oh hadst thou, Cruel! been content to seize
Hairs less in sight, or any Hairs but these!

Part 5

SHE said: the pitying Audience melt in Tears,
But *Fate* and *Jove* had stopp'd the *Baron*'s Ears.
In vain *Thalestris* with Reproach assails,
For who can move when fair *Belinda* fails?
Not half to fixt the *Trojan* cou'd remain,
While *Anna* begg'd and *Dido* rag'd in vain.
Then grave *Clarissa* graceful wav'd her Fan;
Silence ensu'd, and thus the Nymph began.
Say, why are Beauties prais'd and honour'd most,
The wise Man's Passion, and the vain Man's Toast?
Why deck'd with all that Land and Sea afford,
Why Angels call'd, and Angel-like ador'd?
Why round our Coaches crowd the white-glov'd Beaus,
Why bows the Side-box from its inmost Rows?
How vain are all these Glories, all our Pains,
Unless good Sense preserve what Beauty gains:
That Men may say, when we the Front-box grace,
Behold the first in Virtue, as in Face!
Oh! if to dance all Night, and dress all Day,
Charm'd the Small-pox, or chas'd old Age away;
Who would not scorn what Huswife's Cares produce,
Or who would learn one earthly Thing of Use?
To patch, nay ogle, might become a Saint,
Nor could it sure be such a Sin to paint.
But since, alas! frail Beauty must decay,
Curl'd or uncurl'd, since Locks will turn to grey,
Since paint'd, or not paint'd, all shall fade,
And she who scorns a Man, must die a Maid;
What then remains, but well our Pow'r to use,
And keep good Humour still whate'er we lose?
And trust me, Dear! good Humour can prevail,
When Airs, and Flights, and Screams, and Scolding fail.
Beauties in vain their pretty Eyes may roll;
Charms strike the Sight, but Merit wins the Soul.
So spake the Dame, but no Applause ensu'd;
Belinda frown'd, *Thalestris* call'd her Prude.
To Arms, to Arms! the fierce Virago cries,
And swift as Lightning to the Combate flies.
All side in Parties, and begin th' Attack;
Fans clap, Silks russle, and tough Whalebones crack;
Heroes and Heroins Shouts confus'dly rise,
And base, and treble Voices strike the Skies.
No common Weapons in their Hands are found,
Like Gods they fight, nor dread a mortal Wound.
So when bold *Homer* makes the Gods engage,
And heav'nly Breasts with human Passions rage;
'Gainst *Pallas, Mars; Latona, Hermes* arms;
And all *Olympus* rings with loud Alarms.
Jove's Thunder roars, Heav'n trembles all around;
Blue *Neptune* storms, the bellowing Deeps resound;
Earth shakes her nodding Tow'rs, the Ground gives way;
And the pale Ghosts start at the Flash of Day!

Triumphant *Umbriel* on a Sconce's Height
Clapt his glad Wings, and sate to view the Fight,
Propt on their Bodkin Spears, the Sprights survey
The growing Combat, or assist the Fray.
While thro' the Press enrag'd *Thalestris* flies,
And scatters Deaths around from both her Eyes,
A *Beau* and *Witling* perish'd in the Throng,
One dy'd in *Metaphor*, and one in *Song*.
O cruel Nymph! a living Death I bear,
Cry'd *Dapperwit*, and sunk beside his Chair.
A mournful Glance Sir *Fopling* upwards cast,
Those Eyes are made so killing---was his last:
Thus on *Meander*'s flow'ry Margin lies
Th' expiring Swan, and as he sings he dies.
When bold Sir *Plume* had drawn *Clarissa* down,
Chloe stept in, and kill'd him with a Frown;
She smil'd to see the doughty Hero slain,
But at her Smile, the Beau reviv'd again.
Now *Jove* suspends his golden Scales in Air,
Weighs the Mens Wits against the Lady's Hair;
The doubtful Beam long nods from side to side;
At length the Wits mount up, the Hairs subside.
See fierce *Belinda* on the *Baron* flies,
With more than usual Lightning in her Eyes;
Nor fear'd the Chief th' unequal Fight to try,
Who sought no more than on his Foe to die.
But this bold Lord, with manly Strength indu'd,
She with one Finger and a Thumb subdu'd,
Just where the Breath of Life his Nostrils drew,
A Charge of *Snuff* the wily Virgin threw;
The *Gnomes* direct, to ev'ry Atome just,
The pungent Grains of titillating Dust.
Sudden, with starting Tears each Eye o'erflows,
And the high Dome re-ecchoes to his Nose.
Now meet thy Fate, incens'd *Belinda* cry'd,
And drew a deadly *Bodkin* from her Side.
(The same, his ancient Personage to deck,
Her great great Grandsire wore about his Neck
In three *Seal-Rings* which after, melted down,
Form'd a vast *Buckle* for his Widow's Gown:
Her infant Grandame's *Whistle* next it grew,
The *Bells* she gingled, and the *Whistle* blew;
Then in a *Bodkin* grac'd her Mother's Hairs,
Which long she wore, and now *Belinda* wears.)
Boast not my Fall (he cry'd) insulting Foe!
Thou by some other shalt be laid as low.
Nor think, to die dejects my lofty Mind;
All that I dread, is leaving you behind!
Rather than so, ah let me still survive,
And burn in *Cupid*'s Flames, but burn alive.
Restore the Lock! she cries; and all around
Restore the Lock! the vaulted Roofs rebound.

Not fierce *Othello* in so loud a Strain
Roar'd for the Handkerchief that caus'd his Pain.
But see how oft Ambitious Aims are cross'd,
And Chiefs contend 'till all the Prize is lost!
The Lock, obtain'd with Guilt, and kept with Pain,
In ev'ry place is sought, but sought in vain:
With such a Prize no Mortal must be blest,
So Heav'n decrees! with Heav'n who can contest?
Some thought it mounted to the Lunar Sphere,
Since all things lost on Earth, are treasur'd there.
There Heroe's Wits are kept in pondrous Vases,
And Beau's in *Snuff-boxes* and *Tweezer-Cases*.
There broken Vows, and Death-bed Alms are found,
And Lovers Hearts with Ends of Riband bound;
The Courtiers Promises, and Sick Man's Pray'rs,
The Smiles of Harlots, and the Tears of Heirs,
Cages for Gnats, and Chains to Yoak a Flea;
Dry'd Butterflies, and Tomes of Casuistry.
But trust the Muse she saw it upward rise,
Tho' mark'd by none but quick Poetic Eyes:
(So *Rome*'s great Founder to the Heav'ns withdrew,
To *Proculus* alone confess'd in view.)
A sudden Star, it shot thro' liquid Air,
And drew behind a radiant *Trail of Hair*.
Not *Berenice*'s Locks first rose so bright,
The heav'ns bespangling with dishevel'd light.
The *Sylphs* behold it kindling as it flies,
And pleas'd pursue its Progress thro' the Skies.
This the *Beau-monde* shall from the *Mall* survey,
And hail with Musick its propitious Ray.
This, the blest Lover shall for *Venus* take,
And send up Vows from *Rosamonda*'s Lake.
This *Partridge* soon shall view in cloudless Skies,
When next he looks thro' *Galilaeo*'s Eyes;
And hence th' Egregious Wizard shall foredoom
The Fate of *Louis*, and the Fall of *Rome*.
Then cease, bright Nymph! to mourn the ravish'd Hair
Which adds new Glory to the shining Sphere!
Not all the Tresses that fair Head can boast
Shall draw such Envy as the Lock you lost.
For, after all the Murders of your Eye,
When, after Millions slain, your self shall die;
When those fair Suns shall sett, as sett they must,
And all those Tresses shall be laid in Dust;
This Lock, the Muse shall consecrate to Fame,
And mid'st the Stars inscribe *Belinda*'s Name!

Summer by Alexander Pope
See what delights in sylvan scenes appear!
Descending Gods have found Elysium here.
In woods bright Venus with Adonis stray'd,

And chaste Diana haunts the forest shade.
Come lovely nymph, and bless the silent hours,
When swains from shearing seek their nightly bow'rs;
When weary reapers quit the sultry field,
And crown'd with corn, their thanks to Ceres yield.
This harmless grove no lurking viper hides,
But in my breast the serpent Love abides.
Here bees from blossoms sip the rosy dew,
But your Alexis knows no sweets but you.
Oh deign to visit our forsaken seats,
The mossy fountains, and the green retreats!
Where-e'er you walk, cool gales shall fan the glade,
Trees, where you sit, shall crowd into a shade,
Where-e'er you tread, the blushing flow'rs shall rise,
And all things flourish where you turn your eyes.
Oh! How I long with you to pass my days,
Invoke the muses, and resound your praise;
Your praise the birds shall chant in ev'ry grove,
And winds shall waft it to the pow'rs above.
But wou'd you sing, and rival Orpheus' strain,
The wond'ring forests soon shou'd dance again,
The moving mountains hear the pow'rful call,
And headlong streams hang list'ning in their fall!
But see, the shepherds shun the noon-day heat,
The lowing herds to murm'ring brooks retreat,
To closer shades the panting flocks remove,
Ye Gods! And is there no relief for Love?
But soon the sun with milder rays descends
To the cool ocean, where his journey ends;
On me Love's fiercer flames for ever prey,
By night he scorches, as he burns by day.

Elergy Written In A Country Churchyard by Thomas Gray
The curfew tolls the knell of parting day,
The lowing herd winds slowly o'er the lea,
The ploughman homeward plods his weary way,
And leaves the world to darkness and to me.

Now fades the glimmering landscape on the sight,
And all the air a solemn stillness holds,
Save where the beetle wheels his droning flight,
And drowsy tinklings lull the distant folds:

Save that from yonder ivy-mantled tower
The moping owl does to the moon complain
Of such as, wandering near her secret bower,
Molest her ancient solitary reign.

Beneath those rugged elms, that yew-tree's shade,
Where heaves the turf in many a mouldering heap,
Each in his narrow cell for ever laid,

The rude Forefathers of the hamlet sleep.

The breezy call of incense-breathing morn,
The swallow twittering from the straw-built shed,
The cock's shrill clarion, or the echoing horn,
No more shall rouse them from their lowly bed.

For them no more the blazing hearth shall burn,
Or busy housewife ply her evening care:
No children run to lisp their sire's return,
Or climb his knees the envied kiss to share,

Oft did the harvest to their sickle yield,
Their furrow oft the stubborn glebe has broke;
How jocund did they drive their team afield!
How bow'd the woods beneath their sturdy stroke!

Let not Ambition mock their useful toil,
Their homely joys, and destiny obscure;
Nor Grandeur hear with a disdainful smile
The short and simple annals of the Poor.

The boast of heraldry, the pomp of power,
And all that beauty, all that wealth e'er gave,
Awaits alike th' inevitable hour:-
The paths of glory lead but to the grave.

Nor you, ye Proud, impute to these the fault
If Memory o'er their tomb no trophies raise,
Where through the long-drawn aisle and fretted vault
The pealing anthem swells the note of praise.

Can storied urn or animated bust
Back to its mansion call the fleeting breath?
Can Honour's voice provoke the silent dust,
Or Flattery soothe the dull cold ear of Death?

Perhaps in this neglected spot is laid
Some heart once pregnant with celestial fire;
Hands, that the rod of empire might have sway'd,
Or waked to ecstasy the living lyre:

But Knowledge to their eyes her ample page,
Rich with the spoils of time, did ne'er unroll;
Chill Penury repress'd their noble rage,
And froze the genial current of the soul.

Full many a gem of purest ray serene
The dark unfathom'd caves of ocean bear:
Full many a flower is born to blush unseen,
And waste its sweetness on the desert air.

Some village-Hampden, that with dauntless breast
The little tyrant of his fields withstood,
Some mute inglorious Milton here may rest,
Some Cromwell, guiltless of his country's blood.

Th' applause of list'ning senates to command,
The threats of pain and ruin to despise,
To scatter plenty o'er a smiling land,
And read their history in a nation's eyes,

Their lot forbad: nor circumscribed alone
Their growing virtues, but their crimes confined;
Forbad to wade through slaughter to a throne,
And shut the gates of mercy on mankind,

The struggling pangs of conscious truth to hide,
To quench the blushes of ingenuous shame,
Or heap the shrine of Luxury and Pride
With incense kindled at the Muse's flame.

Far from the madding crowd's ignoble strife,
Their sober wishes never learn'd to stray;
Along the cool sequester'd vale of life
They kept the noiseless tenour of their way.

Yet e'en these bones from insult to protect
Some frail memorial still erected nigh,
With uncouth rhymes and shapeless sculpture deck'd,
Implores the passing tribute of a sigh.

Their name, their years, spelt by th' unletter'd Muse,
The place of fame and elegy supply:
And many a holy text around she strews,
That teach the rustic moralist to die.

For who, to dumb forgetfulness a prey,
This pleasing anxious being e'er resign'd,
Left the warm precincts of the cheerful day,
Nor cast one longing lingering look behind?

On some fond breast the parting soul relies,
Some pious drops the closing eye requires;
E'en from the tomb the voice of Nature cries,
E'en in our ashes live their wonted fires.

For thee, who, mindful of th' unhonour'd dead,
Dost in these lines their artless tale relate;
If chance, by lonely contemplation led,
Some kindred spirit shall inquire thy fate,

Haply some hoary-headed swain may say,
Oft have we seen him at the peep of dawn

Brushing with hasty steps the dews away,
To meet the sun upon the upland lawn;

'There at the foot of yonder nodding beech
That wreathes its old fantastic roots so high.
His listless length at noontide would he stretch,
And pore upon the brook that babbles by.

'Hard by yon wood, now smiling as in scorn,
Muttering his wayward fancies he would rove;
Now drooping, woeful wan, like one forlorn,
Or crazed with care, or cross'd in hopeless love.

'One morn I miss'd him on the custom'd hill,
Along the heath, and near his favourite tree;
Another came; nor yet beside the rill,
Nor up the lawn, nor at the wood was he;

'The next with dirges due in sad array
Slow through the church-way path we saw him borne,
Approach and read (for thou canst read) the lay
Graved on the stone beneath yon aged thorn.'

The Epitaph
Here rests his head upon the lap of Earth
A youth to Fortune and to Fame unknown.
Fair Science frowned not on his humble birth,
And Melacholy marked him for her own.

Large was his bounty, and his soul sincere,
Heaven did a recompense as largely send:
He gave to Misery all he had, a tear,
He gained from Heaven ('twas all he wish'd) a friend.

No farther seek his merits to disclose,
Or draw his frailties from their dread abode
(There they alike in trembling hope repose),
The bosom of his Father and his God.

The Lamb by William Blake
Little Lamb who made thee
Dost thou know who made thee
Gave thee life & bid thee feed
By the stream & o'er the mead;
Gave thee clothing of delight,
Softest clothing woolly bright;
Gave thee such a tender voice,
Making all the vales rejoice!
Little Lamb who made thee
Dost thou know who made thee

Little Lamb I'll tell thee,
Little Lamb I'll tell thee!
He is called by thy name,
For he calls himself a Lamb:
He is meek & he is mild,
He became a little child:
I a child & thou a lamb,
We are called by his name.
Little Lamb God bless thee.
Little Lamb God bless thee.

The Tiger by William Blake

Tyger! Tyger! burning bright
In the forests of the night,
What immortal hand or eye
Could frame thy fearful symmetry?

In what distant deeps or skies
Burnt the fire of thine eyes?
On what wings dare he aspire?
What the hand dare sieze the fire?
And what shoulder, & what art.
Could twist the sinews of thy heart?
And when thy heart began to beat,
What dread hand? & what dread feet?
What the hammer? what the chain?
In what furnace was thy brain?
What the anvil? what dread grasp
Dare its deadly terrors clasp?
When the stars threw down their spears,
And watered heaven with their tears,
Did he smile his work to see?
Did he who made the Lamb make thee?
Tyger! Tyger! burning bright
In the forests of the night,
What immortal hand or eye
Dare frame thy fearful symmetry?

How Sweet I Roam'd From Field To Field by William Blake

How sweet I roam'd from field to field,
And tasted all the summer's pride
'Til the prince of love beheld
Who in the sunny beams did glide!

He shew'd me lilies for my hair
And blushing roses for my brow;
He led me through his garden fair,
Where all his golden pleasures grow.

With sweet May dews my wings were wet,

And Phoebus fir'd my vocal rage
He caught me in his silken net,
And shut me in his golden cage.

He loves to sit and hear me sing,
Then, laughing, sports and plays with me;
Then stretches out my golden wing,
And mocks my loss of liberty.

Composed Upon Westminster Bridge by William Wordsworth
Earth has not anything to show more fair:
Dull would he be of soul who could pass by
A sight so touching in its majesty:
This City now doth, like a garment, wear
The beauty of the morning; silent, bare,
Ships, towers, domes, theatres, and temples lie
Open unto the fields, and to the sky;
All bright and glittering in the smokeless air.
Never did sun more beautifully steep
In his first splendour, valley, rock, or hill;
Ne'er saw I, never felt, a calm so deep!
The river glideth at his own sweet will:
Dear God! the very houses seem asleep;
And all that mighty heart is lying still!

Daffodils by William Wordsworth
I wandered lonely as a cloud
That floats on high o'er vales and hills,
When all at once I saw a crowd,
A host, of golden daffodils;
Beside the lake, beneath the trees,
Fluttering and dancing in the breeze.

Continuous as the stars that shine
And twinkle on the milky way,
They stretched in never-ending line
Along the margin of a bay:
Ten thousand saw I at a glance,
Tossing their heads in sprightly dance.

The waves beside them danced; but they
Out-did the sparkling waves in glee:
A poet could not but be gay,
In such a jocund company:
I gazed and gazed but little thought
What wealth the show to me had brought:

For oft, when on my couch I lie
In vacant or in pensive mood,
They flash upon that inward eye

Which is the bliss of solitude;
And then my heart with pleasure fills,
And dances with the daffodils.

Departing summer hath assumed
An aspect tenderly illumed,
The gentlest look of spring;
That calls from yonder leafy shade
Unfaded, yet prepared to fade,
A timely carolling.

No faint and hesitating trill,
Such tribute as to winter chill
The lonely redbreast pays!
Clear, loud, and lively is the din,
From social warblers gathering in
Their harvest of sweet lays.

Nor doth the example fail to cheer
Me, conscious that my leaf is sere,
And yellow on the bough:—
Fall, rosy garlands, from my head!
Ye myrtle wreaths, your fragrance shed
Around a younger brow!

Yet will I temperately rejoice;
Wide is the range, and free the choice
Of undiscordant themes;
Which, haply, kindred souls may prize
Not less than vernal ecstasies,
And passion's feverish dreams.

For deathless powers to verse belong,
And they like Demi-gods are strong
On whom the Muses smile;
But some their function have disclaimed,
Best pleased with what is aptliest framed
To enervate and defile.

Not such the initiatory strains
Committed to the silent plains
In Britain's earliest dawn:
Trembled the groves, the stars grew pale,
While all-too-daringly the veil
Of nature was withdrawn!

Nor such the spirit-stirring note
When the live chords Alcæus smote,
Inflamed by sense of wrong;
Woe! woe to Tyrants! from the lyre

Broke threateningly, in sparkles dire
Of fierce vindictive song.

And not unhallowed was the page
By wingèd Love inscribed, to assuage
The pangs of vain pursuit;
Love listening while the Lesbian Maid
With finest touch of passion swayed
Her own Æolian lute.

O ye, who patiently explore
The wreck of Herculanean lore,
What rapture! could ye seize
Some Theban fragment, or unroll
One precious, tender-hearted scroll
Of pure Simonides.

That were, indeed, a genuine birth
Of poesy; a bursting forth
Of genius from the dust:
What Horace gloried to behold,
What Maro loved, shall we enfold?
Can haughty Time be just!

Frost At Midnight by Samuel Taylor Coleridge
The Frost performs its secret ministry,
Unhelped by any wind. The owlet's cry
Came loud—and hark, again! loud as before.
The inmates of my cottage, all at rest,
Have left me to that solitude, which suits
Abstruser musings: save that at my side
My cradled infant slumbers peacefully.
'Tis calm indeed! so calm, that it disturbs
And vexes meditation with its strange
And extreme silentness. Sea, hill, and wood,
This populous village! Sea, and hill, and wood,
With all the numberless goings-on of life,
Inaudible as dreams! the thin blue flame
Lies on my low-burnt fire, and quivers not;
Only that film, which fluttered on the grate,

Still flutters there, the sole unquiet thing.
Methinks, its motion in this hush of nature
Gives it dim sympathies with me who live,
Making it a companionable form,
Whose puny flaps and freaks the idling Spirit
By its own moods interprets, every where
Echo or mirror seeking of itself,
And makes a toy of Thought.

But O! how oft,

How oft, at school, with most believing mind,
Presageful, have I gazed upon the bars,
To watch that fluttering *stranger* ! and as oft
With unclosed lids, already had I dreamt
Of my sweet birth-place, and the old church-tower,
Whose bells, the poor man's only music, rang
From morn to evening, all the hot Fair-day,
So sweetly, that they stirred and haunted me
With a wild pleasure, falling on mine ear
Most like articulate sounds of things to come!
So gazed I, till the soothing things, I dreamt,
Lulled me to sleep, and sleep prolonged my dreams!
And so I brooded all the following morn,
Awed by the stern preceptor's face, mine eye
Fixed with mock study on my swimming book:
Save if the door half opened, and I snatched
A hasty glance, and still my heart leaped up,
For still I hoped to see the *stranger's* face,
Townsman, or aunt, or sister more beloved,
My play-mate when we both were clothed alike!

Dear Babe, that sleepest cradled by my side,
Whose gentle breathings, heard in this deep calm,
Fill up the interspersèd vacancies
And momentary pauses of the thought!
My babe so beautiful! it thrills my heart
With tender gladness, thus to look at thee,
And think that thou shalt learn far other lore,
And in far other scenes! For I was reared
In the great city, pent 'mid cloisters dim,
And saw nought lovely but the sky and stars.
But *thou*, my babe! shalt wander like a breeze
By lakes and sandy shores, beneath the crags
Of ancient mountain, and beneath the clouds,
Which image in their bulk both lakes and shores
And mountain crags: so shalt thou see and hear
The lovely shapes and sounds intelligible
Of that eternal language, which thy God
Utters, who from eternity doth teach
Himself in all, and all things in himself.
Great universal Teacher! he shall mould
Thy spirit, and by giving make it ask.

Therefore all seasons shall be sweet to thee,
Whether the summer clothe the general earth
With greenness, or the redbreast sit and sing
Betwixt the tufts of snow on the bare branch
Of mossy apple-tree, while the nigh thatch
Smokes in the sun-thaw; whether the eave-drops fall
Heard only in the trances of the blast,
Or if the secret ministry of frost
Shall hang them up in silent icicles,

Quietly shining to the quiet Moon.

Work Without Hope by Samuel Taylor Coleridge
All Nature seems at work. Slugs leave their lair—
The bees are stirring—birds are on the wing—
And Winter slumbering in the open air,
Wears on his smiling face a dream of Spring!
And I the while, the sole unbusy thing,
Nor honey make, nor pair, nor build, nor sing.

Yet well I ken the banks where amaranths blow,
Have traced the fount whence streams of nectar flow.
Bloom, O ye amaranths! bloom for whom ye may,
For me ye bloom not! Glide, rich streams, away!
With lips unbrightened, wreathless brow, I stroll:
And would you learn the spells that drowse my soul?
Work without Hope draws nectar in a sieve,
And Hope without an object cannot live.

Ozymandias by Shelley
I met a Traveler from an antique land,
Who said, "Two vast and trunkless legs of stone
Stand in the desart. Near them, on the sand,
Half sunk, a shattered visage lies, whose frown,
And wrinkled lip, and sneer of cold command,
Tell that its sculptor well those passions read,
Which yet survive, stamped on these lifeless things,
The hand that mocked them and the heart that fed:
And on the pedestal these words appear:
"My name is OZYMANDIAS, King of Kings."
Look on my works ye Mighty, and despair!
No thing beside remains. Round the decay
Of that Colossal Wreck, boundless and bare,
The lone and level sands stretch far away.

Ode To The West Wind by Shelley
I.
Wild West Wind, thou breath of Autumn's being,
Thou, from whose unseen presence the leaves dead
Are driven, like ghosts from an enchanter fleeing,

Yellow, and black, and pale, and hectic red,
Pestilence-stricken multitudes: O thou,
Who chariotest to their dark wintry bed

The wingèd seeds, where they lie cold and low,
Each like a corpse within its grave, until
Thine azure sister of the spring shall blow

Her clarion o'er the dreaming earth, and fill
(Driving sweet buds like flocks to feed in air)
With living hues and odors plain and hill:

Wild Spirit, which art moving everywhere;
Destroyer and preserver; hear, oh, hear!

II.
Thou on whose stream, 'mid the steep sky's commotion,
Loose clouds like earth's decaying leaves are shed,
Shook from the tangled boughs of Heaven and Ocean,

Angels of rain and lightning: there are spread
On the blue surface of thine airy surge,
Like the bright hair uplifted from the head

Of some fierce Mænad, even from the dim verge
Of the horizon to the zenith's height,
The locks of the approaching storm. Thou dirge

Of the dying year, to which this closing night
Will be the dome of a vast sepulchre,
Vaulted with all thy congregated might

Of vapors, from whose solid atmosphere
Black rain, and fire, and hail, will burst: oh hear!

III.
Thou who didst waken from his summer dreams
The blue Mediterranean, where he lay,
Lulled by the coil of his crystalline streams,

Beside a pumice isle in Baiæ's bay,
And saw in sleep old palaces and towers
Quivering within the wave's intenser day,

All overgrown with azure moss and flowers
So sweet, the sense faints picturing them! Thou
For whose path the Atlantic's level powers

Cleave themselves into chasms, while far below
The sea-blooms and the oozy woods which wear
The sapless foliage of the ocean, know

Thy voice, and suddenly grow gray with fear,
And tremble and despoil themselves: oh, hear!

IV.
If I were a dead leaf thou mightest bear;
If I were a swift cloud to fly with thee;
A wave to pant beneath thy power, and share

The impulse of thy strength, only less free
Than thou, O uncontrollable! if even
I were as in my boyhood, and could be

The comrade of thy wanderings over heaven,
As then, when to outstrip thy skyey speed
Scarce seemed a vision; I would ne'er have striven

As thus with thee in prayer in my sore need.
Oh! lift me as a wave, a leaf, a cloud!
I fall upon the thorns of life! I bleed!

A heavy weight of hours has chained and bowed
One too like thee: tameless, and swift, and proud.

V.
Make me thy lyre, even as the forest is;
What if my leaves are falling like its own!
The tumult of thy mighty harmonies

Will take from both a deep, autumnal tone,
Sweet though in sadness. Be thou, Spirit fierce,
My spirit! Be thou me, impetuous one!

Drive my dead thoughts over the universe
Like withered leaves to quicken a new birth!
And, by the incantation of this verse,

Scatter, as from an extinguished hearth
Ashes and sparks, my words among mankind!
Be through my lips to unwakened earth

The trumpet of a prophecy! O Wind,
If Winter comes, can Spring be far behind?

Short Extract From Prometheus Unbound by Shelley
Monarch of Gods and Dæmons, and all Spirits
But One, who throng those bright and rolling worlds
Which Thou and I alone of living things
Behold with sleepless eyes! regard this Earth
Made multitudinous with thy slaves, whom thou
Requitest for knee-worship, prayer, and praise,
And toil, and hecatombs of broken hearts,
With fear and self-contempt and barren hope.
Whilst me, who am thy foe, eyeless in hate,
Hast thou made reign and triumph, to thy scorn,
O'er mine own misery and thy vain revenge.
Three thousand years of sleep-unsheltered hours,
And moments aye divided by keen pangs
Till they seemed years, torture and solitude,

Scorn and despair,—these are mine empire:—
More glorious far than that which thou surveyest
From thine unenvied throne, O Mighty God!
Almighty, had I deigned to share the shame
Of thine ill tyranny, and hung not here
Nailed to this wall of eagle-baffling mountain,
Black, wintry, dead, unmeasured; without herb,
Insect, or beast, or shape or sound of life.
Ah me! alas, pain, pain ever, for ever!

No change, no pause, no hope! Yet I endure.
I ask the Earth, have not the mountains felt?
I ask yon Heaven, the all-beholding Sun,
Has it not seen? The Sea, in storm or calm,
Heaven's ever-changing Shadow, spread below,
Have its deaf waves not heard my agony?
Ah me! alas, pain, pain ever, for ever!

The crawling glaciers pierce me with the spears
Of their moon-freezing crystals, the bright chains
Eat with their burning cold into my bones.
Heaven's wingèd hound, polluting from thy lips
His beak in poison not his own, tears up
My heart; and shapeless sights come wandering by,
The ghastly people of the realm of dream,
Mocking me: and the Earthquake-fiends are charged
To wrench the rivets from my quivering wounds
When the rocks split and close again behind:
While from their loud abysses howling throng
The genii of the storm, urging the rage
Of whirlwind, and afflict me with keen hail.
And yet to me welcome is day and night,
Whether one breaks the hoar frost of the morn,
Or starry, dim, and slow, the other climbs
The leaden-coloured east; for then they lead
The wingless, crawling hours, one among whom
As some dark Priest hales the reluctant victim
Shall drag thee, cruel King, to kiss the blood
From these pale feet, which then might trample thee
If they disdained not such a prostrate slave.
Disdain! Ah no! I pity thee. What ruin
Will hunt thee undefended through wide Heaven!
How will thy soul, cloven to its depth with terror,
Gape like a hell within! I speak in grief,
Not exultation, for I hate no more,
As then ere misery made me wise. The curse
Once breathed on thee I would recall. Ye Mountains,
Whose many-voicèd Echoes, through the mist
Of cataracts, flung the thunder of that spell!
Ye icy Springs, stagnant with wrinkling frost,
Which vibrated to hear me, and then crept
Shuddering through India! Thou serenest Air,

Through which the Sun walks burning without beams!
And ye swift Whirlwinds, who on poisèd wings
Hung mute and moveless o'er yon hushed abyss,
As thunder, louder than your own, made rock
The orbèd world! If then my words had power,
Though I am changed so that aught evil wish
Is dead within; although no memory be
Of what is hate, let them not lose it now!
What was that curse? for ye all heard me speak.

I Am by John Clare

I am: yet what I am none cares or knows,
My friends forsake me like a memory lost;
I am the self-consumer of my woes,
They rise and vanish in oblivious host,
Like shades in love and death's oblivion lost;
And yet I am! and live with shadows tost

Into the nothingness of scorn and noise,
Into the living sea of waking dreams,
Where there is neither sense of life nor joys,
But the vast shipwreck of my life's esteems;
And e'en the dearest--that I loved the best
Are strange nay, rather stranger than the rest.

I long for scenes where man has never trod;
A place where woman never smil'd or wept;
There to abide with my creator, God,
And sleep as I in childhood sweetly slept:
Untroubling and untroubled where I lie;
The grass below--above the vaulted sky.

Ode To A Nightingale by John Keats

My heart aches, and a drowsy numbness pains
My sense, as though of hemlock I had drunk,
Or emptied some dull opiate to the drains
One minute past, and Lethe-wards had sunk:
'Tis not through envy of thy happy lot,
But being too happy in thine happiness, -
That thou, light-winged Dryad of the trees,
In some melodious plot
Of beechen green and shadows numberless,
Singest of summer in full-throated ease.
O, for a draught of vintage! that hath been
Cool'd a long age in the deep-delved earth,
Tasting of Flora and the country green,
Dance, and Provençal song, and sunburnt mirth!
O for a beaker full of the warm South,
Full of the true, the blushful Hippocrene,
With beaded bubbles winking at the brim,

And purple-stained mouth;
That I might drink, and leave the world unseen,
And with thee fade away into the forest dim:
Fade far away, dissolve, and quite forget
What thou among the leaves hast never known,
The weariness, the fever, and the fret
Here, where men sit and hear each other groan;
Where palsy shakes a few, sad, last gray hairs,
Where youth grows pale, and spectre-thin, and dies;
Where but to think is to be full of sorrow
And leaden-eyed despairs,
Where Beauty cannot keep her lustrous eyes,
Or new Love pine at them beyond to-morrow.
Away! away! for I will fly to thee,
Not charioted by Bacchus and his pards,
But on the viewless wings of Poesy,
Though the dull brain perplexes and retards:
Already with thee! tender is the night,
And haply the Queen-Moon is on her throne,
Cluster'd around by all her starry Fays;
But here there is no light,
Save what from heaven is with the breezes blown
Through verdurous glooms and winding mossy ways.
I cannot see what flowers are at my feet,
Nor what soft incense hangs upon the boughs,
But, in embalmed darkness, guess each sweet
Wherewith the seasonable month endows
The grass, the thicket, and the fruit-tree wild;
White hawthorn, and the pastoral eglantine;
Fast fading violets cover'd up in leaves;
And mid-May's eldest child,
The coming musk-rose, full of dewy wine,
The murmurous haunt of flies on summer eves.
Darkling I listen; and, for many a time
I have been half in love with easeful Death,
Call'd him soft names in many a mused rhyme,
To take into the air my quiet breath;
Now more than ever seems it rich to die,
To cease upon the midnight with no pain,
While thou art pouring forth thy soul abroad
In such an ecstasy!
Still wouldst thou sing, and I have ears in vain
To thy high requiem become a sod.
Thou wast not born for death, immortal Bird!
No hungry generations tread thee down;
The voice I hear this passing night was heard
In ancient days by emperor and clown:
Perhaps the self-same song that found a path
Through the sad heart of Ruth, when, sick for home,
She stood in tears amid the alien corn;
The same that oft-times hath

Charm'd magic casements, opening on the foam
Of perilous seas, in faery lands forlorn.
Forlorn! the very word is like a bell
To toll me back from thee to my sole self!
Adieu! the fancy cannot cheat so well
As she is fam'd to do, deceiving elf.
Adieu! adieu! thy plaintive anthem fades
Past the near meadows, over the still stream,
Up the hill-side; and now 'tis buried deep
In the next valley-glades:
Was it a vision, or a waking dream?
Fled is that music: - Do I wake or sleep?

Ode To Autumn by John Keats

Season of mists and mellow fruitfulness!
Close bosom-friend of the maturing sun;
Conspiring with him how to load and bless
With fruit the vines that round the thatch-eaves run;
To bend with apples the mossed cottage-trees,
And fill all fruit with ripeness to the core;
To swell the gourd, and plump the hazel shells
With a sweet kernel; to set budding more,
And still more, later flowers for the bees,
Until they think warm days will never cease,
For Summer has o'erbrimmed their clammy cells.

Who hath not seen thee oft amid thy store?
Sometimes whoever seeks abroad may find
Thee sitting careless on a granary floor,
Thy hair soft-lifted by the winnowing wind;
Or on a half-reaped furrow sound asleep,
Drowsed with the fume of poppies, while thy hook
Spares the next swath and all its twined flowers;
And sometimes like a gleaner thou dost keep
Steady thy laden head across a brook;
Or by a cider-press, with patient look,
Thou watchest the last oozings, hours by hours.

Where are the songs of Spring? Ay, where are they?
Think not of them, thou hast thy music too, -
While barred clouds bloom the soft-dying day
And touch the stubble-plains with rosy hue;
Then in a wailful choir the small gnats mourn
Among the river sallows, borne aloft
Or sinking as the light wind lives or dies;
And full-grown lambs loud bleat from hilly bourn;
Hedge-crickets sing, and now with treble soft
The redbreast whistles from a garden-croft;
And gathering swallows twitter in the skies.

Bright Star by John Keats

Bright star, would I were stedfast as thou art
Not in lone splendour hung aloft the night
And watching, with eternal lids apart,
Like nature's patient, sleepless Eremite,
The moving waters at their priestlike task
Of pure ablution round earth's human shores,
Or gazing on the new soft-fallen mask
Of snow upon the mountains and the moors
No--yet still stedfast, still unchangeable,
Pillow'd upon my fair love's ripening breast,
To feel for ever its soft fall and swell,
Awake for ever in a sweet unrest,
Still, still to hear her tender-taken breath,
And so live ever-or else swoon to death.

La Belle Dame Sans Merci by John Keats

O what can ail thee, knight-at-arms,
Alone and palely loitering?
The sedge has withered from the lake,
And no birds sing.

O what can ail thee, knight-at-arms,
So haggard and so woe-begone?
The squirrel's granary is full,
And the harvest's done.

I see a lily on thy brow,
With anguish moist and fever-dew,
And on thy cheeks a fading rose
Fast withereth too.

I met a lady in the meads,
Full beautiful—a faery's child,
Her hair was long, her foot was light,
And her eyes were wild.

I made a garland for her head,
And bracelets too, and fragrant zone;
She looked at me as she did love,
And made sweet moan

I set her on my pacing steed,
And nothing else saw all day long,
For sidelong would she bend, and sing
A faery's song.

She found me roots of relish sweet,
And honey wild, and manna-dew,
And sure in language strange she said—
'I love thee true'.

She took me to her Elfin grot,
And there she wept and sighed full sore,
And there I shut her wild wild eyes
With kisses four.

And there she lullèd me asleep,
And there I dreamed—Ah! woe betide!—
The latest dream I ever dreamt
On the cold hill side.

I saw pale kings and princes too,
Pale warriors, death-pale were they all;
They cried—'La Belle Dame sans Merci
Thee hath in thrall!'

I saw their starved lips in the gloam,
With horrid warning gapèd wide,
And I awoke and found me here,
On the cold hill's side.

And this is why I sojourn here,
Alone and palely loitering,
Though the sedge is withered from the lake,
And no birds sing.

I Remember I Remember by Thomas Hood

I remember, I remember
The house where I was born,
The little window where the sun
Came peeping in at morn;
He never came a wink too soon
Nor brought too long a day;
But now, I often wish the night
Had borne my breath away.

I remember, I remember
The roses red and white,
The violets and the lily cups
Those flowers made of light!
The lilacs where the robin built,
And where my brother set
The laburnum on his birthday,
The tree is living yet!

I remember, I remember
Where I was used to swing,
And thought the air must rush as fresh
To swallows on the wing;
My spirit flew in feathers then
That is so heavy now,

The summer pools could hardly cool
The fever on my brow.

I remember, I remember
The fir-trees dark and high;
I used to think their slender tops
Were close against the sky:
It was a childish ignorance,
But now 'tis little joy
To know I'm farther off from Heaven
Than when I was a boy.

Ballad by Thomas Hood
Spring it is cheery,
Winter is dreary,
Green leaves hang, but the brown must fly;
When he 's forsaken,
Wither'd and shaken,
What can an old man do but die?

Love will not clip him,
Maids will not lip him,
Maud and Marian pass him by;
Youth it is sunny,
Age has no honey,
What can an old man do but die?

June it was jolly,
O for its folly!
A dancing leg and a laughing eye;
Youth may be silly,
Wisdom is chilly,
What can an old man do but die?

Friends they are scanty,
Beggars are plenty,
If he has followers, I know why;
Gold 's in his clutches,
(Buying him crutches!)
What can an old man do but die?

No! by Thomas Hood
No sun-no moon!
No morn-no noon!
No dawn-no dusk-no proper time of day
No sky-no earthly view
No distance looking blue
No road-no street-no "t'other side this way"
No end to any Row
No indications where the Crescents go

No top to any steeple
No recognitions of familiar people
No courtesies for showing 'em
No knowing 'em!
No traveling at all-no locomotion
No inkling of the way-no notion
"No go" by land or ocean
No mail-no post
No news from any foreign coast
No Park, no Ring, no afternoon gentility
No company-no nobility
No warmth, no cheerfulness, no healthful ease,
No comfortable feel in any member
No shade, no shine, no butterflies, no bees,
No fruits, no flowers, no leaves, no birds
November!

If Thou Must Love Me by Elizabeth Barrett Browning

If thou must love me, let it be for nought
Except for love's sake only. Do not say
`I love her for her smile ...her look...her way
Of speaking gently, for a trick of thought
That falls in well with mine, and certes brought
A sense of pleasant ease on such a day'
For these things in themselves, Beloved, may
Be changed, or change for thee,and love, so wrought,
May be unwrought so. Neither love me for
Thine own dear pity's wiping my cheeks dry,
A creature might forget to weep, who bore
Thy comfort long, and lose thy love thereby!
But love me for love's sake, that evermore
Thou may'st love on, through love's eternity.

How Do I Love Thee by Elizabeth Barrett Browning

How do I love thee? Let me count the ways.
I love thee to the depth and breadth and height
My soul can reach, when feeling out of sight
For the ends of being and ideal grace.
I love thee to the level of every day's
Most quiet need, by sun and candle-light.
I love thee freely, as men strive for right.
I love thee purely, as they turn from praise.
I love thee with the passion put to use
In my old griefs, and with my childhood's faith.
I love thee with a love I seemed to lose
With my lost saints. I love thee with the breath,
Smiles, tears, of all my life; and, if God choose,
I shall but love thee better after death.

Ulysses by Alfred Lord Tennyson

It little profits that an idle king,
By this still hearth, among these barren crags,
Match'd with an aged wife, I mete and dole
Unequal laws unto a savage race,
That hoard, and sleep, and feed, and know not me.
I cannot rest from travel; I will drink
Life to the lees. All times I have enjoy'd
Greatly, have suffer'd greatly, both with those
That loved me, and alone; on shore, and when
Thro' scudding drifts the rainy Hyades
Vext the dim sea. I am become a name;
For always roaming with a hungry heart
Much have I seen and known, cities of men
And manners, climates, councils, governments,
Myself not least, but honor'd of them all,
And drunk delight of battle with my peers,
Far on the ringing plains of windy Troy.
I am a part of all that I have met;
Yet all experience is an arch wherethro'
Gleams that untravell'd world whose margin fades
For ever and for ever when I move.
How dull it is to pause, to make an end,
To rust unburnish'd, not to shine in use!
As tho' to breathe were life! Life piled on life
Were all too little, and of one to me
Little remains; but every hour is saved
>From that eternal silence, something more,
A bringer of new things; and vile it were
For some three suns to store and hoard myself,
And this gray spirit yearning in desire
To follow knowledge like a sinking star,
Beyond the utmost bound of human thought.
This is my son, mine own Telemachus,
to whom I leave the sceptre and the isle,
Well-loved of me, discerning to fulfill
This labor, by slow prudence to make mild
A rugged people, and thro' soft degrees
Subdue them to the useful and the good.
Most blameless is he, centred in the sphere
Of common duties, decent not to fail
In offices of tenderness, and pay
Meet adoration to my household gods,
When I am gone. He works his work, I mine.
There lies the port; the vessel puffs her sail;
There gloom the dark, broad seas. My mariners,
Souls that have toil'd, and wrought, and thought with me,
That ever with a frolic welcome took
The thunder and the sunshine, and opposed
Free hearts, free foreheads, you and I are old;
Old age hath yet his honor and his toil.
Death closes all; but something ere the end,

Some work of noble note, may yet be done,
Not unbecoming men that strove with Gods.
The lights begin to twinkle from the rocks;
The long day wanes; the slow moon climbs; the deep
Moans round with many voices. Come, my friends.
'T is not too late to seek a newer world.
Push off, and sitting well in order smite
The sounding furrows; for my purpose holds
To sail beyond the sunset, and the baths
Of all the western stars, until I die.
It may be that the gulfs will wash us down;
It may be we shall touch the Happy Isles,
And see the great Achilles, whom we knew.
Tho' much is taken, much abides; and tho'
We are not now that strength which in old days
Moved earth and heaven, that which we are, we are,
One equal temper of heroic hearts,
Made weak by time and fate, but strong in will
To strive, to seek, to find, and not to yield.

Lady Clare by Alfred Lord Tennyson
It was the time when lilies blow,
And clouds are highest up in air.
Lord Ronald brought a lily-white doe
To give his cousin, Lady Clare.
I trow they did not part in scorn:
Lovers long betrothed were they;
They two will wed the morrow morn;
God's blessing on the day!
"He does not love me for my birth
Nor for my lands so broad and fair;
He loves me for my own true worth,
And that is well," said Lady Clare.
In there came old Alice the nurse,
Said, "Who was this that went from thee?"
"It was my cousin," said Lady Clare;
"To-morrow he weds with me."
"Oh, God be thanked!" said Alice the nurse,
"That all comes round so just and fair:
Lord Ronald is heir of all your lands,
And you are not the Lady Clare."
"Are ye out of your mind, my nurse, my nurse,"
Said Lady Clare, "that ye speak so wild?"
"As God's above," said Alice the nurse,
"I speak the truth: you are my child.
The old earl's daughter died at my breast;
I speak the truth, as I live by bread!
I buried her like my own sweet child,
And put my child in her stead."
"Falsely, falsely have ye done,
O mother," she said, "if this be true,

To keep the best man under the sun
So many years from his due."
"Nay now, my child," said Alice the nurse,
"But keep the secret for your life,
And all you have will be Lord Ronald's,
When you are man and wife."
"If I'm a beggar born," she said
"I will speak out, for I dare not lie,
Pull off, pull off the brooch of gold,
And fling the diamond necklace by."
"Nay now, my child," said Alice the nurse,
"But keep the secret all you can."
She said, "Not so; but I will know
If there be any faith in man."
"Nay now, what faith?" said Alice the nurse,
"The man will cleave unto his right."
"And he shall have it," the lady replied,
"Though I should die to-night."
"Yet give one kiss to your mother, dear!
Alas, my child! I sinned for thee."
"O mother, mother, mother," she said,
"So strange it seems to me!
"Yet here's a kiss for my mother dear,
My mother dear, if this be so,
And lay your hand upon my head,
And bless me, mother, ere I go."
She clad herself in a russen gown,
She was no longer Lady Clare:
She went by dale, and she went by down,
With a single rose in her hair.
The lily-white doe Lord Ronald had brought
Leapt up from where she lay.
Dropped her head in the maiden's hand.
And followed her all the way.
Down stepped Lord Ronald from his tower:
"O Lady Clare, you shame your worth!
Why come you dressed like a village maid,
That are the flower of the earth?"
"If I come dressed like a village maid,
I am but as my fortunes are:
I am a begger born," she said,
"And not the Lady Clare."
"Play me no tricks," said Lord Ronald,
"For I am yours in word and in deed;
Play me no tricks," said Lord Ronald,
"Your riddle is hard to read."
Oh, and proudly stood she up!
Her heart within her did not fail:
She looked into Lord Ronald's eyes,
And told him all her nurse's tale.
He laughed a laugh of merry scorn:
He turned and kissed her where she stood;

"If you are not the heiress born,
And I," said he, "the next in blood--
"If you are not the heiress born,
And I," said he, "the lawful heir,
We two will wed to-morrow morn,
And you shall still be Lady Clare."

Pied Piper Of Hamblin by Robert Browning

I

Hamelin Town's in Brunswick,
By famous Hanover city;
The river Weser, deep and wide,
Washes its wall on the southern side;
A pleasanter spot you never spied;
But, when begins my ditty,
Almost five hundred years ago,
To see the townsfolk suffer so
From vermin, was a pity.

II

Rats!
They fought the dogs and killed the cats,
And bit the babies in the cradles,
And ate the cheeses out of the vats,
And licked the soup from the cooks' own ladle's,
Split open the kegs of salted sprats,
Made nests inside men's Sunday hats,
And even spoiled the women's chats
By drowning their speaking
With shrieking and squeaking
In fifty different sharps and flats.

III

At last the people in a body
To the town hall came flocking:
"'Tis clear," cried they, 'our Mayor's a noddy;
And as for our Corporation-shocking
To think we buy gowns lined with ermine
For dolts that can't or won't determine
What's best to rid us of our vermin!
You hope, because you're old and obese,
To find in the furry civic robe ease?
Rouse up, sirs! Give your brains a racking
To find the remedy we're lacking,
Or, sure as fate, we'll send you packing!"
At this the Mayor and Corporation
Quaked with a mighty consternation.

IV

An hour they sat in council,
At length the Mayor broke silence:

"For a guilder I'd my ermine gown sell,
I wish I were a mile hence!
It's easy to bid one rack one's brain
I'm sure my poor head aches again,
I've scratched it so, and all in vain
Oh for a trap, a trap, a trap!"
Just as he said this, what should hap
At the chamber door but a gentle tap?
"Bless us,' cried the Mayor, "what's that?"
(With the Corporation as he sat,
Looking little though wondrous fat;
Nor brighter was his eye, nor moister
Than a too-long-opened oyster,
Save when at noon his paunch grew mutinous
For a plate of turtle, green and glutinous)
"Only a scraping of shoes on the mat?
Anything like the sound of a rat
Makes my heart go pit-a-pat!"

V

"Come in!" the Mayor cried, looking bigger:
And in did come the strangest figure!
His queer long coat from heel to head
Was half of yellow and half of red
And he himself was tall and thin,
With sharp blue eyes, each like a pin,
And light loose hair, yet swarthy skin,
No tuft on cheek nor beard on chin,
But lips where smiles went out and in--
There was no guessing his kith and kin!
And nobody could enough admire
The tall man and his quaint attire.
Quoth one: "It's as if my great-grandsire,
Starting up at the Trump of Doom's tone,
Had walked this way from his painted tombstone!"

VI

He advanced to the council-table:
And, "Please your honors," said he, "I'm able,
By means of a secret charm, to draw
All creatures living beneath the sun,
That creep or swim or fly or run,
After me so as you never saw!
And I chiefly use my charm
On creatures that do people harm,
The mole and toad and newt and viper;
And people call me the Pied Piper."
(And here they noticed round his neck
A scarf of red and yellow stripe,
To match with his coat of the self-same check;
And at the scarf's end hung a pipe;
And his fingers, they noticed, were ever straying

As if impatient to be playing
Upon this pipe, as low it dangled
Over his vesture so old-fangled.)
"Yet," said he, "poor piper as I am,
In Tartary I freed the Cham,
Last June, from his huge swarm of gnats;
I eased in Asia the Nizam
Of a monstrous brood of vampyre-bats:
And as for what your brain bewilders--
If I can rid your town of rats
Will you give me a thousand guilders?"
"One? Fifty thousand!" was the exclamation
Of the astonished Mayor and Corporation.

VII
Into the street the Piper stept,
Smiling first a little smile,
As if he knew what magic slept
In his quiet pipe the while;
Then, like a musical adept,
To blow the pipe his lips he wrinkled,
And green and blue his sharp eyes twinkled,
Like a candle-flame where salt is sprinkled;
And ere three shrill notes the pipe uttered,
You heard as if an army muttered;
And the muttering grew to a grumbling;
And the grumbling grew to a mighty rumbling;
And out of the houses the rats came tumbling.
Great rats, small rats, lean rats, brawny rats,
Brown rats, black rats, gray rats, tawny rats,
Grave old plodders, gay young friskers,
Fathers, mothers, uncles, cousins,
Cocking tails and pricking whiskers,
Families by tens and dozens,
Brothers, sisters, husbands, wives--
Followed the Piper for their lives.
From street to street he piped advancing,
And step for step they followed dancing,
Until they came to the river Weser
Wherein all plunged and perished!
‹Save one who, stout as Julius Caesar,
Swam across and lived to carry
(As the manuscript he cherished)
To Rat-land home his commentary:
Which was, "At the first shrill notes of the pipe,
I heard a sound as of scraping tripe,
And putting apples, wondrous ripe,
Into a cider-press's gripe:
And a moving away of pickle-tub-boards,
And a leaving ajar of conserve-cupboards,
And a drawing the corks of train-oil-flasks,
And a breaking the hoops of butter-casks:

And it seemed as if a voice
(Sweeter far than by harp or by psaltery
Is breathed) called out, 'Oh rats, rejoice!
The world is grown to one vast dry-saltery!
So munch on, crunch on, take your nuncheon,
Breakfast, supper, dinner, luncheon!'
And just as a bulky sugar-puncheon,
All ready staved, like a great sun shone
Glorious scarce an inch before me,
Just as methought it said 'Come bore me!'
I found the Weser rolling o'er me."

VIII

You should have heard the Hamelin people
Ringing the bells till they rocked the steeple.
Go," cried the Mayor, "and get long poles!
Poke out the nests and block up the holes!
Consult with carpenters and builders
And leave in our town not even a trace
Of the rats!"-- when suddenly, up the face
Of the Piper perked in the market-place,
With a, "First, if you please, my thousand guilders!"

IX

A thousand guilders! The Mayor looked blue;
So did the Corporation too.
For council dinners made rare havoc
With Claret, Moselle, Vin-de-Grave, Hock;
And half the money would replenish
Their cellar's biggest butt with Rhenish.
To pay this sum to a wandering fellow
With a gypsy coat of red and yellow!
"Beside," quoth the Mayor with a knowing wink,
"Our business was done at the river's brink;
We saw with our eyes the vermin sink,
And what's dead can't come to life, I think.
So, friend, we're not the folks to shrink
From the duty of giving you something for drink,
And a matter of money to put in your poke;
But as for the guilders, what we spoke
Of them, as you very well know, was in joke.
Beside, our losses have made us thrifty.
A thousand guilders! Come, take fifty!

X

The Piper's face fell, and he cried,
"No trifling! I can't wait! Beside,
I've promised to visit by dinnertime
Bagdad, and accept the prime
Of the Head-Cook's pottage, all he's rich in,
For having left, in the Caliph's kitchen,
Of a nest of scorpions no survivor

With him I proved no bargain-driver,
With you, don't think I'll bate a stiver!
And folks who put me in a passion
May find me pipe to another fashion."

XI

"How?" cried the Mayor, "d'ye think I brook
Being worse treated than a Cook?
Insulted by a lazy ribald
With idle pipe and vesture piebald?
You threaten us, fellow? Do your worst,
Blow your pipe there till you burst!"

XII

Once more he stept into the street
And to his lips again
Laid his long pipe of smooth straight cane;
And ere he blew three notes (such sweet
Soft notes as yet musician's cunning
Never gave the enraptured air)
There was a rustling that seemed like a bustling
Of merry crowds justling at pitching and hustling,
Small feet were pattering, wooden shoes clattering,
Little hands clapping, and little tongues chattering,
And, like fowls in a farm-yard when barley is scattering,
Out came the children running.
All the little boys and girls,
With rosy cheeks and flaxen curls,
And sparkling eyes and teeth like pearls,
Tripping and skipping, ran merrily after
The wonderful music with shouting and laughter.

XIII

The Mayor was dumb, and the Council stood
As if they were changed into blocks of wood,
Unable to move a step or cry,
To the children merrily skipping by--
And could only follow with the eye
That joyous crowd at the Piper's back.
But how the Mayor was on the rack
And the wretched Council's bosoms beat,
As the Piper turned from the High Street
To where the Weser rolled its water's
Right in the way of their sons and daughters!
However he turned from South to West
And to Koppelberg Hill his steps addressed,
And after him the children pressed;
Great was the joy in every breast.
"He never can cross that mighty top!
He's forced to let the piping drop
And we shall see our children stop!
When, lo, as they reached the mountain-side,

A wondrous portal opened wide,
As if a cavern was suddenly hollowed;
And the Piper advanced and the children followed,
And when all were in to the very last,
The door in the mountain-side shut fast.
Did I say all? No! One was lame,
And could not dance the whole of the way;
And in after years, if you would blame
His sadness, he was used to say,
"It's dull in our town since my playmates left!
I can't forget that I'm bereft
Of all the pleasant sights they see,
Which the Piper also promised me.
For he led us, he said, to a joyous land,
Joining the town and just at hand,
Where waters gushed and fruit-trees grew,
And flowers put forth a fairer hue,
And everything was strange and new;
The sparrows were brighter than peacocks here,
And their dogs outran our fallow deer,
And honey-bees had lost their stings,
And horses were born with eagles' wings:
And just as I became assured
My lame foot would be speedily cured,
The music stopped and I stood still,
And found myself outside the hill,
Left alone against my will,
To go now limping as before,
And never hear of that country more!

XIV
Alas, alas for Hamelin!
There came into many a burgher's pate
A text which says that heaven's gate
Opens to the rich at as easy rate
As the needle's eye takes a camel in!
The mayor sent East, West, North and South,
To offer the Piper, by word of mouth
Wherever it was men's lot to find him,
Silver and gold to his heart's content,
If he'd only return the way he went,
And bring the children behind him.
But when they saw 'twas a lost endeavor,
And Piper and dancers were gone forever,
They made a decree that lawyers never
Should think their records dated duly
If, after the day of the month and year,
These words did not as well appear:
"And so long after what happened here
On the twenty-second of July,
Thirteen hundred and seventy-six;"
And the better in memory to fix

The place of the children's last retreat,
They called it the Pied Piper's Street,
Where any one playing on pipe or tabor
Was sure for the future to lose his labor.
Nor suffered they hostelry or tavern
To shock with mirth a street so solemn,
But opposite the place of the cavern
They wrote the story on a column,
And on the great church-window painted
The same, to make the world acquainted
How their children were stolen away,
And there it stands to this very day.
And I must not omit to say
That, in Transylvania there's a tribe
Of alien people who ascribe
To the outlandish ways and dress
On which their neighbors lay such stress,
To their fathers and mothers having risen
Out of some subterranean prison
Into which they were trepanned
Long time ago in a mighty band
Out of Hamelin town in Brunswick land,
But how or why they don't understand.

XV

So, Willy, let you and me be wipers
Of scores out with all men--especially pipers!
And, whether they pipe us free, from rats or from mice,
If we've promised them ought, let us keep our promise.

Home Thoughts From Abroad by Robert Browning

Oh, to be in England
Now that April's there,
And whoever wakes in England
Sees, some morning, unaware,
That the lowest boughs and the brushwood sheaf
Round the elm-tree bole are in tiny leaf,
While the chaffinch sings on the orchard bough
In England—now!

And after April, when May follows,
And the whitethroat builds, and all the swallows!
Hark, where my blossomed pear-tree in the hedge
Leans to the field and scatters on the clover
Blossoms and dewdrops—at the bent spray's edge—
That's the wise thrush; he sings each song twice over,
Lest you should think he never could recapture
The first fine careless rapture!
And though the fields look rough with hoary dew,
All will be gay when noontide wakes anew
The buttercups, the little children's dower

—Far brighter than this gaudy melon-flower!

I
They went to sea in a Sieve, they did,
In a Sieve they went to sea:
In spite of all their friends could say,
On a winter's morn, on a stormy day,
In a Sieve they went to sea!
And when the Sieve turned round and round,
And every one cried, 'You'll all be drowned!'
They called aloud, 'Our Sieve ain't big,
But we don't care a button! we don't care a fig!
In a Sieve we'll go to sea!'
Far and few, far and few,
Are the lands where the Jumblies live;
Their heads are green, and their hands are blue,
And they went to sea in a Sieve.

II
They sailed away in a Sieve, they did,
In a Sieve they sailed so fast,
With only a beautiful pea-green veil
Tied with a riband by way of a sail,
To a small tobacco-pipe mast;
And every one said, who saw them go,
'O won't they be soon upset, you know!
For the sky is dark, and the voyage is long,
And happen what may, it's extremely wrong
In a Sieve to sail so fast!'
Far and few, far and few,
Are the lands where the Jumblies live;
Their heads are green, and their hands are blue,
And they went to sea in a Sieve.

III
The water it soon came in, it did,
The water it soon came in;
So to keep them dry, they wrapped their feet
In a pinky paper all folded neat,
And they fastened it down with a pin.
And they passed the night in a crockery-jar,
And each of them said, 'How wise we are!
Though the sky be dark, and the voyage be long,
Yet we never can think we were rash or wrong,
While round in our Sieve we spin!'
Far and few, far and few,
Are the lands where the Jumblies live;
Their heads are green, and their hands are blue,
And they went to sea in a Sieve.

IV

And all night long they sailed away;
And when the sun went down,
They whistled and warbled a moony song
To the echoing sound of a coppery gong,
In the shade of the mountains brown.
'O Timballo! How happy we are,
When we live in a sieve and a crockery-jar,
And all night long in the moonlight pale,
We sail away with a pea-green sail,
In the shade of the mountains brown!'
Far and few, far and few,
Are the lands where the Jumblies live;
Their heads are green, and their hands are blue,
And they went to sea in a Sieve.

V

They sailed to the Western Sea, they did,
To a land all covered with trees,
And they bought an Owl, and a useful Cart,
And a pound of Rice, and a Cranberry Tart,
And a hive of silvery Bees.
And they bought a Pig, and some green Jack-daws,
And a lovely Monkey with lollipop paws,
And forty bottles of Ring-Bo-Ree,
And no end of Stilton Cheese.
Far and few, far and few,
Are the lands where the Jumblies live;
Their heads are green, and their hands are blue,
And they went to sea in a Sieve.

VI

And in twenty years they all came back,
In twenty years or more,
And every one said, 'How tall they've grown!'
For they've been to the Lakes, and the Torrible Zone,
And the hills of the Chankly Bore;
And they drank their health, and gave them a feast
Of dumplings made of beautiful yeast;
And everyone said, 'If we only live,
We too will go to sea in a Sieve,
To the hills of the Chankly Bore!'
Far and few, far and few,
Are the lands where the Jumblies live;
Their heads are green, and their hands are blue,
And they went to sea in a Sieve.

Dover Beach by Matthew Arnold

The sea is calm to-night.
The tide is full, the moon lies fair
Upon the straits; on the French coast the light

Gleams and is gone; the cliffs of England stand,
Glimmering and vast, out in the tranquil bay.
Come to the window, sweet is the night-air!
Only, from the long line of spray
Where the sea meets the moon-blanch'd land,
Listen! you hear the grating roar
Of pebbles which the waves draw back, and fling,
At their return, up the high strand,
Begin, and cease, and then again begin,
With tremulous cadence slow, and bring
The eternal note of sadness in.

Sophocles long ago
Heard it on the Aegean, and it brought
Into his mind the turbid ebb and flow
Of human misery; we
Find also in the sound a thought,
Hearing it by this distant northern sea.

The Sea of Faith
Was once, too, at the full, and round earth's shore
Lay like the folds of a bright girdle furl'd.
But now I only hear
Its melancholy, long, withdrawing roar,
Retreating, to the breath
Of the night-wind, down the vast edges drear
And naked shingles of the world.

Ah, love, let us be true
To one another! for the world, which seems
To lie before us like a land of dreams,
So various, so beautiful, so new,
Hath really neither joy, nor love, nor light,
Nor certitude, nor peace, nor help for pain;
And we are here as on a darkling plain
Swept with confused alarms of struggle and flight,
Where ignorant armies clash by night.

Remember by Christina Georgina Rossetti
Remember me when I am gone away,
Gone far away into the silent land;
When you can no more hold me by the hand,
Nor I half turn to go yet turning stay.
Remember me when no more day by day
You tell me of our future that you plann'd:
Only remember me; you understand
It will be late to counsel then or pray.
Yet if you should forget me for a while
And afterwards remember, do not grieve:
For if the darkness and corruption leave
A vestige of the thoughts that once I had,

Better by far you should forget and smile
Than that you should remember and be sad.

In The Willow Shade by Christina Georgina Rossetti
I sat beneath a willow tree,
Where water falls and calls;
While fancies upon fancies solaced me,
Some true, and some were false.

Who set their heart upon a hope
That never comes to pass,
Droop in the end like fading heliotrope
The sun's wan looking-glass.

Who set their will upon a whim
Clung to through good and ill,
Are wrecked alike whether they sink or swim,
Or hit or miss their will.

All things are vain that wax and wane,
For which we waste our breath;
Love only doth not wane and is not vain,
Love only outlives death.

A singing lark rose toward the sky,
Circling he sang amain;
He sang, a speck scarce visible sky-high,
And then he sank again.

A second like a sunlit spark
Flashed singing up his track;
But never overtook that foremost lark,
And songless fluttered back.

A hovering melody of birds
Haunted the air above;
They clearly sang contentment without words,
And youth and joy and love.

O silvery weeping willow tree
With all leaves shivering,
Have you no purpose but to shadow me
Beside this rippled spring?

On this first fleeting day of Spring,
For Winter is gone by,
And every bird on every quivering wing
Floats in a sunny sky;

On this first Summer-like soft day,
While sunshine steeps the air,

And every cloud has gat itself away,
And birds sing everywhere.

Have you no purpose in the world
But thus to shadow me
With all your tender drooping twigs unfurled,
O weeping willow tree?

With all your tremulous leaves outspread
Betwixt me and the sun,
While here I loiter on a mossy bed
With half my work undone;

My work undone, that should be done
At once with all my might;
For after the long day and lingering sun
Comes the unworking night.

This day is lapsing on its way,
Is lapsing out of sight;
And after all the chances of the day
Comes the resourceless night.

The weeping willow shook its head
And stretched its shadow long;
The west grew crimson, the sun smoldered red,
The birds forbore a song.

Slow wind sighed through the willow leaves,
The ripple made a moan,
The world drooped murmuring like a thing that grieves;
And then I felt alone.

I rose to go, and felt the chill,
And shivered as I went;
Yet shivering wondered, and I wonder still,
What more that willow meant;

That silvery weeping willow tree
With all leaves shivering,
Which spent one long day overshadowing me
Beside a spring in Spring.

The Oxen by Thomas Hardy
Christmas Eve, and twelve of the clock.
"Now they are all on their knees,"
An elder said as we sat in a flock
By the embers in hearthside ease.

We pictured the meek mild creatures where
They dwelt in their strawy pen,

Nor did it occur to one of us there
To doubt they were kneeling then.

So fair a fancy few would weave
In these years! Yet, I feel,
If someone said on Christmas Eve,
"Come; see the oxen kneel

"In the lonely barton by yonder coomb
Our childhood used to know,"
I should go with him in the gloom,
Hoping it might be so.

Ah Are You Digging My Grave by Thomas Hardy

"Ah, are you digging on my grave,
My loved one? — planting rue?"
"No: yesterday he went to wed
One of the brightest wealth has bred.
'It cannot hurt her now,' he said,
'That I should not be true.'"

"Then who is digging on my grave,
My nearest dearest kin?"
"Ah, no: they sit and think, 'What use!
What good will planting flowers produce?
No tendance of her mound can loose
Her spirit from Death's gin.'"

"But someone digs upon my grave?
My enemy? — prodding sly?"
— "Nay: when she heard you had passed the Gate
That shuts on all flesh soon or late,
She thought you no more worth her hate,
And cares not where you lie.

"Then, who is digging on my grave?
Say — since I have not guessed!"
— "O it is I, my mistress dear,
Your little dog , who still lives near,
And much I hope my movements here
Have not disturbed your rest?"

"Ah yes! You dig upon my grave…
Why flashed it not to me
That one true heart was left behind!
What feeling do we ever find
To equal among human kind
A dog's fidelity!"

"Mistress, I dug upon your grave
To bury a bone, in case

I should be hungry near this spot
When passing on my daily trot.
I am sorry, but I quite forgot
It was your resting place."

The Darkling Thrush by Thomas Hardy

I leant upon a coppice gate
When Frost was spectre-grey,
And Winter's dregs made desolate
The weakening eye of day.
The tangled bine-stems scored the sky
Like strings of broken lyres,
And all mankind that haunted nigh
Had sought their household fires.

The land's sharp features seemed to be
The Century's corpse outleant,
His crypt the cloudy canopy,
The wind his death-lament.
The ancient pulse of germ and birth
Was shrunken hard and dry,
And every spirit upon earth
Seemed fervourless as I.

At once a voice arose among
The bleak twigs overhead
In a full-hearted evensong
Of joy illimited;
An aged thrush, frail, gaunt, and small,
In blast-beruffled plume,
Had chosen thus to fling his soul
Upon the growing gloom.

So little cause for carolings
Of such ecstatic sound
Was written on terrestrial things
Afar or nigh around,
That I could think there trembled through
His happy good-night air
Some blessed Hope, whereof he knew
And I was unaware.

Loveliest Of Trees, The Cherry Now by A E Houseman

Loveliest of trees, the cherry now
Is hung with bloom along the bough,
And stands about the woodland ride
Wearing white for Eastertide.

Now, of my threescore years and ten,
Twenty will not come again,

And take from seventy springs a score,
It only leaves me fifty more.

And since to look at things in bloom
Fifty springs are little room,
About the woodlands I will go
To see the cherry hung with snow.

If by Rudyard Kipling

If you can keep your head when all about you
Are losing theirs and blaming it on you,
If you can trust yourself when all men doubt you,
But make allowance for their doubting too;
If you can wait and not be tired by waiting,
Or being lied about, don't deal in lies,
Or being hated, don't give way to hating,
And yet don't look too good, nor talk too wise:

If you can dream—and not make dreams your master;
If you can think—and not make thoughts your aim;
If you can meet with Triumph and Disaster
And treat those two impostors just the same;
If you can bear to hear the truth you've spoken
Twisted by knaves to make a trap for fools,
Or watch the things you gave your life to, broken,
And stoop and build 'em up with worn-out tools:

If you can make one heap of all your winnings
And risk it on one turn of pitch-and-toss,
And lose, and start again at your beginnings
And never breathe a word about your loss;
If you can force your heart and nerve and sinew
To serve your turn long after they are gone,
And so hold on when there is nothing in you
Except the Will which says to them: 'Hold on!'

If you can talk with crowds and keep your virtue,
Or walk with Kings—nor lose the common touch,
If neither foes nor loving friends can hurt you,
If all men count with you, but none too much;
If you can fill the unforgiving minute
With sixty seconds' worth of distance run,
Yours is the Earth and everything that's in it,
And—which is more—you'll be a Man, my son!

Tommy by Rudyard Kipling

I went into a public-'ouse to get a pint o' beer,
The publican 'e up an' sez, "We serve no red-coats here."
The girls be'ind the bar they laughed an' giggled fit to die,
I outs into the street again an' to myself sez I:
O it's Tommy this, an' Tommy that, an' "Tommy, go away";

But it's "Thank you, Mister Atkins", when the band begins to play,
The band begins to play, my boys, the band begins to play,
O it's "Thank you, Mister Atkins", when the band begins to play.

I went into a theatre as sober as could be,
They gave a drunk civilian room, but 'adn't none for me;
They sent me to the gallery or round the music-'alls,
But when it comes to fightin', Lord! they'll shove me in the stalls!
For it's Tommy this, an' Tommy that, an' "Tommy, wait outside";
But it's "Special train for Atkins" when the trooper's on the tide,
The troopship's on the tide, my boys, the troopship's on the tide,
O it's "Special train for Atkins" when the trooper's on the tide.

Yes, makin' mock o' uniforms that guard you while you sleep
Is cheaper than them uniforms, an' they're starvation cheap;
An' hustlin' drunken soldiers when they're goin' large a bit
Is five times better business than paradin' in full kit.
Then it's Tommy this, an' Tommy that, an' "Tommy, 'ow's yer soul?"
But it's "Thin red line of 'eroes" when the drums begin to roll,
The drums begin to roll, my boys, the drums begin to roll,
O it's "Thin red line of 'eroes" when the drums begin to roll.

We aren't no thin red 'eroes, nor we aren't no blackguards too,
But single men in barricks, most remarkable like you;
An' if sometimes our conduck isn't all your fancy paints,
Why, single men in barricks don't grow into plaster saints;
While it's Tommy this, an' Tommy that, an' "Tommy, fall be'ind",
But it's "Please to walk in front, sir", when there's trouble in the wind,
There's trouble in the wind, my boys, there's trouble in the wind,
O it's "Please to walk in front, sir", when there's trouble in the wind.

You talk o' better food for us, an' schools, an' fires, an' all:
We'll wait for extry rations if you treat us rational.
Don't mess about the cook-room slops, but prove it to our face
The Widow's Uniform is not the soldier-man's disgrace.
For it's Tommy this, an' Tommy that, an' "Chuck him out, the brute!"
But it's "Saviour of 'is country" when the guns begin to shoot;
An' it's Tommy this, an' Tommy that, an' anything you please;
An' Tommy ain't a bloomin' fool -- you bet that Tommy sees!

The Way That Lovers Use by Rupert Brooke
The way that lovers use is this;
They bow, catch hands, with never a word,
And their lips meet, and they do kiss,
— So I have heard.

They queerly find some healing so,
And strange attainment in the touch;
There is a secret lovers know,
— I have read as much.

And theirs no longer joy nor smart,
Changing or ending, night or day;
But mouth to mouth, and heart on heart,
— So lovers say.

Love by Rupert Brooke
Love is a breach in the walls, a broken gate,
Where that comes in that shall not go again;
Love sells the proud heart's citadel to Fate.
They have known shame, who love unloved. Even then,
When two mouths, thirsty each for each, find slaking,
And agony's forgot, and hushed the crying
Of credulous hearts, in heaven such are but taking
Their own poor dreams within their arms, and lying
Each in his lonely night, each with a ghost.
Some share that night. But they know love grows colder,
Grows false and dull, that was sweet lies at most.
Astonishment is no more in hand or shoulder,
But darkens, and dies out from kiss to kiss.
All this is love; and all love is but this.

The Old Vicarage of Grantchester by Rupert Brooke
Just now the lilac is in bloom,
All before my little room;
And in my flower-beds, I think,
Smile the carnation and the pink;
And down the borders, well I know,
The poppy and the pansy blow
Oh! there the chestnuts, summer through,
Beside the river make for you
A tunnel of green gloom, and sleep
Deeply above; and green and deep
The stream mysterious glides beneath,
Green as a dream and deep as death.
— Oh, damn! I know it! and I know
How the May fields all golden show,
And when the day is young and sweet,
Gild gloriously the bare feet
That run to bathe. . .*Du lieber Gott!*
Here am I, sweating, sick, and hot,
And there the shadowed waters fresh
Lean up to embrace the naked flesh.
Temperamentvoll German Jews
Drink beer around; — and there the dews
Are soft beneath a morn of gold.
Here tulips bloom as they are told;
Unkempt about those hedges blows
An English unofficial rose;
And there the unregulated sun
Slopes down to rest when day is done,

And wakes a vague unpunctual star,
A slippered Hesper; and there are
Meads towards Haslingfield and Coton
Where *das Betreten's* not *verboten*.
eithe genoimen ... would I were
In Grantchester, in Grantchester!
Some, it may be, can get in touch
With Nature there, or Earth, or such.
And clever modern men have seen
A Faun a-peeping through the green,
And felt the Classics were not dead,
To glimpse a Naiad's reedy head,
Or hear the Goat-foot piping low:
But these are things I do not know.
I only know that you may lie
Day long and watch the Cambridge sky,
And, flower-lulled in sleepy grass,
Hear the cool lapse of hours pass,
Until the centuries blend and blur
In Grantchester, in Grantchester.
Still in the dawnlit waters cool
His ghostly Lordship swims his pool,
And tries the strokes, essays the tricks,
Long learnt on Hellespont, or Styx.
Dan Chaucer hears his river still
Chatter beneath a phantom mill.
Tennyson notes, with studious eye,
How Cambridge waters hurry by
And in that garden, black and white,
Creep whispers through the grass all night;
And spectral dance, before the dawn,
A hundred Vicars down the lawn;
Curates, long dust, will come and go
On lissom, clerical, printless toe;
And oft between the boughs is seen
The sly shade of a Rural Dean
Till, at a shiver in the skies,
Vanishing with Satanic cries,
The prim ecclesiastic rout
Leaves but a startled sleeper-out,
Grey heavens, the first bird's drowsy calls,
The falling house that never falls.
God! I will pack, and take a train,
And get me to England once again!
For England's the one land, I know,
Where men with Splendid Hearts may go;
And Cambridgeshire, of all England,
The shire for Men who Understand;
And of that district I prefer
The lovely hamlet Grantchester.
For Cambridge people rarely smile,
Being urban, squat, and packed with guile;

And Royston men in the far South
Are black and fierce and strange of mouth;
At Over they fling oaths at one,
And worse than oaths at Trumpington,
And Ditton girls are mean and dirty,
And there's none in Harston under thirty,
And folks in Shelford and those parts
Have twisted lips and twisted hearts,
And Barton men make Cockney rhymes,
And Coton's full of nameless crimes,
And things are done you'd not believe
At Madingley on Christmas Eve.
Strong men have run for miles and miles,
When one from Cherry Hinton smiles;
Strong men have blanched, and shot their wives,
Rather than send them to St Ives;
Strong men have cried like babes, bydam,
To hear what happened at Babraham.
But Grantchester! ah, Grantchester!
There's peace and holy quiet there,
Great clouds along pacific skies,
And men and women with straight eyes,
Lithe children lovelier than a dream,
A bosky wood, a slumbrous stream,
And little kindly winds that creep
Round twilight corners, half asleep.
In Grantchester their skins are white;
They bathe by day, they bathe by night;
The women there do all they ought;
The men observe the Rules of Thought.
They love the Good; they worship Truth;
They laugh uproariously in youth;
(And when they get to feeling old,
They up and shoot themselves, I'm told)
Ah God! to see the branches stir
Across the moon at Grantchester!
To smell the thrilling-sweet and rotten
Unforgettable, unforgotten
River-smell, and hear the breeze
Sobbing in the little trees.
Say, do the elm-clumps greatly stand
Still guardians of that holy land?
The chestnuts shade, in reverend dream,
The yet unacademic stream?
Is dawn a secret shy and cold
Anadyomene, silver-gold?
And sunset still a golden sea
From Haslingfield to Madingley?
And after, ere the night is born,
Do hares come out about the corn?
Oh, is the water sweet and cool,
Gentle and brown, above the pool?

And laughs the immortal river still
Under the mill, under the mill?
Say, is there Beauty yet to find?
And Certainty? and Quiet kind?
Deep meadows yet, for to forget
The lies, and truths, and pain? . . . oh! yet
Stands the Church clock at ten to three?
And is there honey still for tea?

Chaucer's Prophecy by Geoffrey Chaucer
When priestes failen in their saws,
And lordes turne Godde's laws
Against the right;
And lechery is holden as privy solace,
And robbery as free purchase,
Beware then of ill!
Then shall the Land of Albion
Turne to confusion,
As sometime it befell.

Ora pro Anglia Sancta Maria, quod Thomas Cantuaria.

Sweet Jesus, heaven's King,
Fair and best of all thing,
You bring us out of this mourning,
To come to thee at our ending!

Truth by Geoffrey Chaucer
Fle fro the pres, and dwelle with sothefastnesse,
Suffise thin owen thing, thei it be smal;
For hord hath hate, and clymbyng tykelnesse,
Prees hath envye, and wele blent overal.
Savour no more thanne the byhove schal;
Reule weel thiself, that other folk canst reede;
And trouthe schal delyvere, it is no drede.

Tempest the nought al croked to redresse,
In trust of hire that tourneth as a bal.
Myche wele stant in litel besynesse;
Bywar therfore to spurne ayeyns an al;
Stryve not as doth the crokke with the wal.
Daunte thiself, that dauntest otheres dede;
And trouthe shal delyvere, it is no drede.

That the is sent, receyve in buxumnesse;
The wrestlyng for the worlde axeth a fal.
Here is non home, here nys but wyldernesse.
Forth, pylgryme, forth! forth, beste, out of thi stal!
Know thi contré! loke up! thonk God of al!
Hold the heye weye, and lat thi gost the lede;

And trouthe shal delyvere, it is no drede.

[L'envoy.]
Therfore, thou Vache, leve thine olde wrechednesse;
Unto the world leve now to be thral.
Crie hym mercy, that of hys hie godnesse
Made the of nought, and in espec{.i}al
Draw unto hym, and pray in general
For the, and eke for other, hevenelyche mede;
And trouthe schal delyvere, it is no drede.

Picture Of Autumn by Thomas Chatterton
When autumn, bleak and sun-burnt, do appear,
With his gold hand gilting the falling leaf,
Bringing up winter to fulfil the year,
Bearing upon his back the riped sheaf;
When all the hills with woody seed are white,
When levying fires, and lemes, do meet from far the sight:
When the fair apple, rudde as even sky,
Do bend the tree unto the fructile ground.
When juicy pears, and berries of black dye,
Do dance in air and call the eyne around;
Then, be the even foul, or even fair,
Methinks my hearte's joy is stained with some care.

The Romance Of The Knight by Thomas Chatterton
The pleasing sweets of spring and summer past,
The falling leaf flies in the sultry blast,
The fields resign their spangling orbs of gold,
The wrinkled grass its silver joys unfold,
Mantling the spreading moor in heavenly white,
Meeting from every hill the ravished sight.
The yellow flag uprears its spotted head,
Hanging regardant o'er its watery bed;
The worthy knight ascends his foaming steed,
Of size uncommon, and no common breed.
His sword of giant make hangs from his belt,
Whose piercing edge his daring foes had felt.
To seek for glory and renown he goes
To scatter death among his trembling foes;
Unnerved by fear, they trembled at his stroke;
So cutting blasts shake the tall mountain oak.

Down in a dark and solitary vale,
Where the curst screech-owl sings her fatal tale,
Where copse and brambles interwoven lie,
Where trees intwining arch the azure sky,
Thither the fate-marked champion bent his way,
By purling streams to lose the heat of day;
A sudden cry assaults his listening ear,

His soul's too noble to admit of fear.-
The cry re-echoes; with his bounding steed
He gropes the way from whence the cries proceed.
The arching trees above obscured the light,
Here 'twas all evening, there eternal night.
And now the rustling leaves and strengthened cry
Bespeaks the cause of the confusion nigh;
Through the thick brake th'astonished champion sees
A weeping damsel bending on her knees:
A ruffian knight would force her to the ground,
But still some small resisting strength she found.
(Women and cats, if you compulsion use,
The pleasure which they die for will refuse.)
The champion thus: 'Desist, discourteous knight,
Why dost thou shamefully misuse thy might?'
With eye contemptuous thus the knight replies,
'Begone! whoever dares my fury dies!'
Down to the ground the champion's gauntlet flew,
'I dare thy fury, and I'll prove it too.'

Like two fierce mountain-boars enraged they fly,
The prancing steeds make Echo rend the sky,
Like a fierce tempest is the bloody fight,
Dead from his lofty steed falls the proud ruffian knight.
The victor, sadly pleased, accosts the dame,
'I will convey you hence to whence you came.'
With look of gratitude the fair replied-
'Content; I in your virtue may confide.
But,' said the fair, as mournful she surveyed
The breathless corse upon the meadow laid,
'May all thy sins from heaven forgiveness find!
May not thy body's crimes affect thy mind!'

The Faerie Queene by Edmund Spenser
THE FIRST BOOKE OF THE FAERIE QUEENE
Contayning
THE LEGENDE OF THE KNIGHT OF THE
RED CROSSE, OR OF HOLINESSE Proemi
Lo I the man, whose Muse whilome did maske,
As time her taught in lowly Shepheards weeds,
Am now enforst a far unfitter taske,
For trumpets sterne to chaunge mine Oaten reeds,
And sing of Knights and Ladies gentle deeds;
Whose prayses having slept in silence long,
Me, all too meane, the sacred Muse areeds
To blazon broad emongst her learned throng:
Fierce warres and faithfull loves shall moralize my song.

ii
Helpe then, O holy Virgin chiefe of nine,

Thy weaker Novice to performe thy will,
Lay forth out of thine everlasting scryne
The antique rolles, which there lye hidden still,
Of Faerie knights and fairest Tanaquill,
Whom that most noble Briton Prince so long
Sought through the world, and suffered so much ill,
That I must rue his undeserved wrong:
O helpe thou my weake wit, and sharpen my dull tong.

iii
And thou most dreaded impe of highest Jove,
Faire Venus sonne, that with thy cruell dart
At that good knight so cunningly didst rove,
That glorious fire it kindled in his hart,
Lay now thy deadly Heben bow apart,
And with thy mother milde come to mine ayde:
Come both, and with you bring triumphant Mart,
In loves and gentle jollities arrayd,
After his murdrous spoiles and bloudy rage allayd.

iv
And with them eke, O Goddesse heavenly bright,
Mirrour of grace and Majestie divine,
Great Lady of the greatest Isle, whose light
Like Phoebus lampe throughout the world doth shine,
Shed thy faire beames into my feeble eyne,
And raise my thoughts too humble and too vile,
To thinke of that true glorious type of thine,
The argument of mine afflicted stile:
The which to heare, vouchsafe, O dearest dred a-while.

A Shepeheards boye (no better doe him call)
when Winters wastful spight was almost spent,
All in a sunneshine day, as did befall,
Led forth his flock, that had been long ypent.
So faynt they woxe, and feeble in the folde,
That now vnnethes their feete could them vphold.

All as the Sheepe, such was the shepeheards looke,
For pale and wanne he was, (alas the while,)
May seeme he lovd, or els some care he tooke:
Well couth he tune his pipe, and frame his stile.
Tho to a hill his faynting flocke he ledde,
And thus him playnd, the while his shepe there fedde.

Ye gods of loue, that pitie louers payne,
(if any gods the paine of louers pitie):
Looke from aboue, where you in ioyes remaine,
And bowe your eares vnto my doleful dittie.
And Pan thou shepheards God, that once didst loue,

Pitie the paines, that thou thy selfe didst proue.

Thou barrein ground, whome winters wrath hath wasted,
Art made a myrrhour, to behold my plight:
Whilome thy fresh spring flowrd, and after hasted
Thy sommer prowde with Daffadillies dight.
And now is come thy wynters stormy state,
Thy mantle mard, wherein thou mas-kedst late.

Such rage as winters, reigneth in my heart,
My life bloud friesing wtih vnkindly cold:
Such stormy stoures do breede my balefull smarte,
As if my yeare were wast, and woxen old.
And yet alas, but now my spring begonne,
And yet alas, yt is already donne.

You naked trees, whose shady leaues are lost,
Wherein the byrds were wont to build their bowre:
And now are clothd with mosse and hoary frost,
Instede of bloosmes, wherwith your buds did flowre:
I see your teares, that from your boughes doe raine,
Whose drops in drery ysicles remaine.

All so my lustfull leafe is drye and sere,
My timely buds with wayling all are wasted:
The blossome, which my braunch of youth did beare,
With breathed sighes is blowne away, & blasted,
And from mine eyes the drizling teares descend,
As on your boughes the ysicles depend.

Thou feeble flocke, whose fleece is rough and rent,
Whose knees are weak through fast and evill fare:
Mayst witnesse well by thy ill gouernement,
Thy maysters mind is ouercome with care.
Thou weak, I wanne: thou leabe, I quite forlorne:
With mourning pyne I, you with pyning mourne.

A thousand sithes I curse that carefull hower,
Wherein I longd the neighbour towne to see:
And eke tenne thousand sithes I blesse the stoure,
Wherein I sawe so fayre a sight, as shee.
Yet all for naught: snch [such] sight hath bred my bane.
Ah God, that loue should breede both ioy and payne.

It is not Hobbinol, wherefore I plaine,
Albee my loue he seeke with dayly suit:
His clownish gifts and curtsies I disdaine,
His kiddes, his cracknelles, and his early fruit.
Ah foolish Hobbinol, thy gyfts bene vayne:
Colin them gives to Rosalind againe.

I loue thilke lasse, (alas why doe I loue?)

And am forlorne, (alas why am I lorne?)
Shee deignes not my good will, but doth reproue,
And of my rurall musick holdeth scorne.
Shepheards deuise she hateth as the snake,
And laughes the songes, that Colin Clout doth make.

Wherefore my pype, albee rude Pan thou please,
Yet for thou pleasest not, where most I would:
And thou vnlucky Muse, that wontst to ease
My musing mynd, yet canst not, when thou should:
Both pype and Muse, shall sore the while abye.
So broke his oaten pype, and downe dyd lye.

By that, the welked Phoebus gan availe,
His weary waine, and nowe the frosty Night
Her mantle black through heauen gan overhaile.
Which seene, the pensife boy halfe in despight
Arose, and homeward drove his sonned sheepe,
Whose hanging heads did seeme his carefull case to weepe.

Heaven by Edward Fairfax
From hence with grace and goodness compass'd round,
God ruleth, blesseth, keepeth all he wrought,
Above the air, the fire, the sea and ground
Our sense, our wit, our reason and our thought;
Where persons three, with power and glory crown'd,
Are all one God, who made all things of naught.
Under whose feet, subjected to his grace
Sit nature, fortune, motion, time and place.

This is the place from whence like smoke and dust
Of this frail world, the wealth, the pomp, the power,
He tosseth, humbleth, turneth as he lust,
And guides our life, our end, our death and hour,
No eye (however virtuous, pure and just)
Can view the brightness of that glorious bower,
On every side the blessed spirits be
Equal in joys though differing in degree.

To The Virgins to Make Much Of Time by Robert Herrick
Gather ye rose-buds while ye may:
Old Time is still a-flying;
And this same flower that smiles to-day,
To-morrow will be dying.

The glorious lamp of heaven, the Sun,
The higher he's a-getting,
The sooner will his race be run,
And nearer he's to setting.

That age is best, which is the first,
When youth and blood are warmer;
But being spent, the worse, and worst
Times, still succeed the former.

Then be not coy, but use your time,
And while ye may, go marry;
For having lost but once your prime,
You may for ever tarry.

A Conjuration To Electra by Robert Herrick
By those soft tods of wool
With which the air is full;
By all those tinctures there,
That paint the hemisphere;
By dews and drizzling rain
That swell the golden grain;
By all those sweets that be
I' the flowery nunnery;
By silent nights, and the
Three forms of Hecate;
By all aspects that bless
The sober sorceress,
While juice she strains, and pith
To make her philters with;
By time that hastens on
Things to perfection;
And by yourself, the best
Conjurement of the rest:
O my Electra! be
In love with none but me.

A Dialogue Between The Soul And Body by Andrew Marvell
Soul
O Who shall, from this Dungeon, raise
A Soul inslav'd so many wayes?
With bolts of Bones, that fetter'd stands
In Feet ; and manacled in Hands.
Here blinded with an Eye ; and there
Deaf with the drumming of an Ear.
A Soul hung up, as 'twere, in Chains
Of Nerves, and Arteries, and Veins.
Tortur'd, besides each other part,1
In a vain Head, and double Heart.

Body
O who shall me deliver whole,
From bonds of this Tyrannic Soul?
Which, stretcht upright, impales me so,
That mine own Precipice I go;

And warms and moves this needless Frame:
(A Fever could but do the same.)
And, wanting where its spight to try,
Has made me live to let me dye.
A Body that could never rest,
Since this ill Spirit it possest.

Soul
What Magic could me thus confine
Within anothers Grief to pine?
Where whatsoever it complain,
I feel, that cannot feel, the pain.
And all my Care its self employes,
That to preserve, which me destroys:
Constrain'd not only to indure
Diseases, but, whats worse, the Cure:
And ready oft the Port to gain,
Am Shipwrackt into Health again.

Body
But Physick yet could never reach
The Maladies Thou me dost teach;
Whom first the Cramp of Hope does Tear:
And then the Palsie Shakes of Fear.
The Pestilence of Love does heat :
Or Hatred's hidden Ulcer eat.
Joy's chearful Madness does perplex:
Or Sorrow's other Madness vex.
Which Knowledge forces me to know;
And Memory will not foregoe.
What but a Soul could have the wit
To build me up for Sin so fit?
So Architects do square and hew,
Green Trees that in the Forest grew.

How wisely Nature did decree,
With the same Eyes to weep and see!
That, having view'd the object vain,
They might be ready to complain.

And since the Self-deluding Sight,
In a false Angle takes each hight;
These Tears which better measure all,
Like wat'ry Lines and Plummets fall.

Two Tears, which Sorrow long did weigh
Within the Scales of either Eye,
And then paid out in equal Poise,
Are the true price of all my Joyes.

What in the World most fair appears,
Yea even Laughter, turns to Tears:
And all the Jewels which we prize,
Melt in these Pendants of the Eyes.

I have through every Garden been,
Amongst the Red,the White, the Green;
And yet, from all the flow'rs I saw,
No Hony, but these Tears could draw.

So the all-seeing Sun each day
Distills the World with Chymick Ray;
But finds the Essence only Showers,
Which straight in pity back he powers.

Yet happy they whom Grief doth bless,
That weep the more, and see the less:
And, to preserve their Sight more true,
Bath still their Eyes in their own Dew.

So Magdalen, in Tears more wise
Dissolv'd those captivating Eyes,
Whose liquid Chains could flowing meet
To fetter her Redeemers feet.

Not full sailes hasting loaden home,
Nor the chast Ladies pregnant Womb,
Nor Cynthia Teeming show's so fair,
As two Eyes swoln with weeping are.

The sparkling Glance that shoots Desire,
Drench'd in these Waves, does lose it fire.
Yea oft the Thund'rer pitty takes
And here the hissing Lightning slakes.

The Incense was to Heaven dear,
Not as a Perfume, but a Tear.
And Stars shew lovely in the Night,
But as they seem the Tears of Light.

Ope then mine Eyes your double Sluice,
And practise so your noblest Use.
For others too can see, or sleep;
But only humane Eyes can weep.

Now like two Clouds dissolving, drop,
And at each Tear in distance stop:
Now like two Fountains trickle down:
Now like two floods o'return and drown.

Thus let your Streams o'reflow your Springs,
Till Eyes and Tears be the same things:

And each the other's difference bears;
These weeping Eyes, those seeing Tears.

Leave Me, O Love Which Reachest But To Dust by Sir Phillip Sidney
Leave me, O love which reachest but to dust,
And thou, my mind, aspire to higher things;
Grow rich in that which never taketh rust:
Whatever fades but fading pleasure brings.
Draw in thy beams, and humble all thy might
To that sweet yoke where lasting freedoms be,
Which breaks the clouds and opens forth the light
That doth both shine and give us sight to see.
O, take fast hold; let that light be thy guide
In this small course which birth draws out to death,
And think how evil becometh him to slide
Who seeketh heaven, and comes of heavenly breath.
Then farewell, world! thy uttermost I see:
Eternal Love, maintain thy life in me.

Sonnet 38 - This Night While Sleep Begins by Sir Phillip Sidney
This night while sleep begins with heavy wings
To hatch mine eyes, and that unbitted thought
Doth fall to stray, and my chief powers are brought
To leave the scepter of all subject things,

The first that straight my fancy's error brings
Unto my mind, is Stella's image, wrought
By Love's own self, but with so curious draught,
That she, methinks, not only shines but sings.

I start, look, hark, but what in clos'd-up sense
Was held, in open'd sense it flies away,
Leaving me nought but wailing eloquence:

I, seeing betters sights in sight's decay,
Call'd it anew, and wooed sleep again:
But him her host that unkind guest had slain.

Vitai Lamparda by Sir Henry Newbolt
There's a breathless hush in the Close to-night
Ten to make and the match to win
A bumping pitch and a blinding light,
An hour to play and the last man in.
And it's not for the sake of a ribboned coat,
Or the selfish hope of a season's fame,
But his Captain's hand on his shoulder smote
"Play up! play up! and play the game!"

The sand of the desert is sodden red,

Red with the wreck of a square that broke;
The Gatling's jammed and the colonel dead,
And the regiment blind with dust and smoke.
The river of death has brimmed his banks,
And England's far, and Honour a name,
But the voice of schoolboy rallies the ranks,
"Play up! play up! and play the game!"

This is the word that year by year
While in her place the School is set
Every one of her sons must hear,
And none that hears it dare forget.
This they all with a joyful mind
Bear through life like a torch in flame,
And falling fling to the host behind
"Play up! play up! and play the game!"

The Life Of Man by Sir Francis Bacon
The world's a bubble; and the life of man less than a span.
In his conception wretched; from the womb so to the tomb:
Curst from the cradle, and brought up to years, with cares and fears.
Who then to frail mortality shall trust,
But limns the water, or but writes in dust.
Yet, since with sorrow here we live oppress'd, what life is best?
Courts are but only superficial schools to dandle fools:
The rural parts are turn'd into a den of savage men:
And where's a city from all vice so free,
But may be term'd the worst of all the three?

Domestic cares afflict the husband's bed, or pains his head:
Those that live single, take it for a curse, or do things worse:
Some would have children; those that have them none; or wish them gone.
What is it then to have no wife, but single thralldom or a double strife?
Our own affections still at home to please, is a disease:
To cross the sea to any foreign soil, perils and toil:
Wars with their noise affright us: when they cease,
We are worse in peace:
What then remains, but that we still should cry,
Not to be born, or being born, to die.

A Poet Of One Mood by Alice Meynell
A poet of one mood in all my lays,
Ranging all life to sing one only love,
Like a west wind across the world I move,
Sweeping my harp of floods mine own wild ways.
The countries change, but not the west-wind days
Which are my songs. My soft skies shine above,
And on all seas the colours of a dove,
And on all fields a flash of silver greys.
I made the whole world answer to my art

And sweet monotonous meanings. In your ears
I change not ever, bearing, for my part,
One thought that is the treasure of my years
A small cloud full of rain upon my heart
And in mine arms, clasped, like a child in tears.

There was a whispering in my hearth,
A sigh of the coal,
Grown wistful of a former earth
It might recall.

I listened for a tale of leaves
And smothered ferns,
Frond-forests, and the low sly lives
Before the fawns.

My fire might show steam-phantoms simmer
From Time's old cauldron,
Before the birds made nests in summer,
Or men had children.

But the coals were murmuring of their mine,
And moans down there
Of boys that slept wry sleep, and men
Writhing for air.

I saw white bones in the cinder-shard,
Bones without number.
For many hearts with coal are charred,
And few remember.

I thought of all that worked dark pits
Of war, and died
Digging the rock where Death reputes
Peace lies indeed:

Comforted years will sit soft-chaired,
In rooms of amber,
The years will stretch their hands, well-cheered
By our life's ember;

The centuries will burn rich loads
With which we groaned,
Whose warmth shall lull their dreaming lids,
While songs are crooned;
But they will not dream of us poor lads
Lost in the ground.

Red lips are not so red
As the stained stones kissed by the English dead.
Kindness of wooed and wooer
Seems shame to their love pure.
O Love, your eyes lose lure
When I behold eyes blinded in my stead!

Your slender attitude
Trembles not exquisite like limbs knife-skewed,
Rolling and rolling there
Where God seems not to care:
Till the fierce love they bear
Cramps them in death's extreme decrepitude.

Your voice sings not so soft,
Though even as wind murmuring through raftered loft,
Your dear voice is not dear,
Gentle, and evening clear,
As theirs whom none now hear,
Now earth has stopped their piteous mouths that coughed.

Heart, you were never hot
Nor large, nor full like hearts made great with shot;
And though your hand be pale,
Paler are all which trail
Your cross through flame and hail:
Weep, you may weep, for you may touch them not.

Sonnet LXII. Off Ostende June 11th 1837 by Henry Alford
But now the level sea-horizon spanned
With its unbroken line the azure round:
I look again, and see the waters crowned
With a pale coronet of distant land;
A shore by us untrodden and unknown,
Thronged with strange men, and voices' stranger sound;
Where we shall wander long, and none be found
To greet with kind salutes and call our own.
Yet even thus, with thee, wife of my love,
Enough the world is peopled; one fond heart
Resting on mine, with others I can part,
Prizing thy gentle excellence above
All native comfort; and, on land or sea,
Then best befriended, if alone with thee.

The Longest Day by William Wordsworth
Let us quit the leafy arbor,
And the torrent murmuring by;
For the sun is in his harbor,
Weary of the open sky.

Evening now unbinds the fetters
Fashioned by the glowing light;
All that breathe are thankful debtors
To the harbinger of night.

Yet by some grave thoughts attended
Eve renews her calm career;
For the day that now is ended,
Is the longest of the year.

Dora! sport, as now thou sportest,
On this platform, light and free;
Take thy bliss, while longest, shortest,
Are indifferent to thee!

Who would check the happy feeling
That inspires the linnet's song?
Who would stop the swallow, wheeling
On her pinions swift and strong?

Yet at this impressive season,
Words which tenderness can speak
From the truths of homely reason,
Might exalt the loveliest cheek;

And, while shades to shades succeeding
Steal the landscape from the sight,
I would urge this moral pleading,
Last forerunner of "Good night!"

Summer ebbs; each day that follows
Is a reflux from on high,
Tending to the darksome hollows
Where the frosts of winter lie.

He who governs the creation,
In his providence, assigned
Such a gradual declination
To the life of human kind.

Yet we mark it not; fruits redden,
Fresh flowers blow, as flowers have blown,
And the heart is loth to deaden
Hopes that she so long hath known.

Be thou wiser, youthful Maiden!
And when thy decline shall come,
Let not dowers, or boughs fruit-laden,
Hide the knowledge of thy doom.

Now, even now, ere wrapped in slumber,
Fix thine eyes upon the sea

That absorbs time, space, and number;
Look thou to Eternity!

Follow thou the flowing river
On whose breast are thither borne
All deceived, and each deceiver,
Through the gates of night and morn;

Through the year's successive portals;
Through the bounds which many a star
Marks, not mindless of frail mortals,
When his light returns from far.

Thus when thou with Time hast travelled
Toward the mighty gulf of things,
And the mazy stream unravelled
With thy best imaginings;

Think, if thou on beauty leanest,
Think how pitiful that stay,
Did not virtue give the meanest
Charms superior to decay.

Duty, like a strict preceptor,
Sometimes frowns, or seems to frown;
Choose her thistle for thy sceptre,
While youth's roses are thy crown.

Grasp it, if thou shrink and tremble,
Fairest damsel of the green,
Thou wilt lack the only symbol
That proclaims a genuine queen;

And ensures those palms of honor
Which selected spirits wear,
Bending low before the Donor,
Lord of heaven's unchanging year!

A Night In June by Alfred Austin
Lady! in this night of June
Fair like thee and holy,
Art thou gazing at the moon
That is rising slowly?
I am gazing on her now:
Something tells me, so art thou.

Night hath been when thou and I
Side by side were sitting,
Watching o'er the moonlit sky
Fleecy cloudlets flitting.
Close our hands were linkèd then;

When will they be linked again?

What to me the starlight still,
Or the moonbeams' splendour,
If I do not feel the thrill
Of thy fingers slender?
Summer nights in vain are clear,
If thy footstep be not near.

Roses slumbering in their sheaths
O'er my threshold clamber,
And the honeysuckle wreathes
Its translucent amber
Round the gables of my home:
How is it thou dost not come?

If thou camest, rose on rose
From its sleep would waken;
From each flower and leaf that blows
Spices would be shaken;
Floating down from star and tree,
Dreamy perfumes welcome thee.

I would lead thee where the leaves
In the moon-rays glisten;
And, where shadows fall in sheaves,
We would lean and listen
For the song of that sweet bird
That in April nights is heard.

And when weary lids would close,
And thy head was drooping,
Then, like dew that steeps the rose,
O'er thy languor stooping,
I would, till I woke a sigh,
Kiss thy sweet lips silently.

I would give thee all I own,
All thou hast would borrow;
I from thee would keep alone
Fear and doubt and sorrow.
All of tender that is mine,
Should most tenderly be thine.

Moonlight! into other skies,
I beseech thee wander.
Cruel, thus to mock mine eyes,
Idle, thus to squander
Love's own light on this dark spot;-
For my lady cometh not!

Remembrance by Emily Bronte

Cold in the earth - and the deep snow piled above thee!
Far, far removed, cold in the dreary grave!
Have I forgot, my only Love, to love thee,
Severed at last by Time's all-severing wave?

Now, when alone, do my thoughts no longer hover
Over the mountains on Angora's shore;
Resting their wings where heath and fern-leaves cover
That noble heart for ever, ever more?

Cold in the earth - and fifteen wild Decembers
From those brown hills have melted into spring:
Faithful, indeed, is the spirit that remembers
After such years of change and suffering!

Sweet Love of youth, forgive, if I forget thee
While the world's tide is bearing me along;
Sterner desires and darker hopes beset me,
Hopes which obscure but cannot do thee wrong.

No other Sun has lightened up my heaven;
No other Star has ever shone for me:
All my life's bliss from thy dear life was given--
All my life's bliss is in the grave with thee.

But when the days of golden dreams had perished
And even Despair was powerless to destroy,
Then did I learn how existence could be cherished,
Strengthened, and fed without the aid of joy;

Then did I check my tears of useless passion -
Weaned my young soul from yearning after thine;
Sternly denied its burning wish to hasten
Down to that tomb already more than mine!

And even yet, I dare not let it languish,
Dare not indulge in Memory's rapturous pain;
Once drinking deep of that divinest anguish,
How could I seek the empty world again?

Despondency by Anne Bronte

I have gone backward in the work,
The labour has not sped,
Drowsy and dark my spirit lies,
Heavy and dull as lead.
How can I rouse my sinking soul
From such a lethargy?
How can I break these iron chains,
And set my spirit free?

There have been times when I have mourned,
In anguish o'er the past;
And raised my suppliant hands on high,
While tears fell thick and fast,

And prayed to have my sins forgiven
With such a fervent zeal,
An earnest grief a strong desire
That now I cannot feel!

And vowed to trample on my sins,
And called on Heaven to aid
My spirit in her firm resolves
And hear the vows I made.

And I have felt so full of love,
So strong in spirit then,
As if my heart would never cool
Or wander back again.

And yet, alas! how many times
My feet have gone astray,
How oft have I forgot my God,
How greatly fallen away!

My sins increase, my love grows cold,
And Hope within me dies,
And Faith itself is wavering now,
O how shall I arise!

I cannot weep but I can pray,
Then let me not despair;
Lord Jesus, save me lest I die,
And hear a wretch's prayer.

Evening Solace by Charlotte Bronte
The human heart has hidden treasures,
In secret kept, in silence sealed;-
The thoughts, the hopes, the dreams, the pleasures,
Whose charms were broken if revealed.
And days may pass in gay confusion,
And nights in rosy riot fly,
While, lost in Fame's or Wealth's illusion,
The memory of the Past may die.

But, there are hours of lonely musing,
Such as in evening silence come,
When, soft as birds their pinions closing,
The heart's best feelings gather home.
Then in our souls there seems to languish
A tender grief that is not woe;

And thoughts that once wrung groans of anguish,
Now cause but some mild tears to flow.

And feelings, once as strong as passions,
Float softly back-a faded dream;
Our own sharp griefs and wild sensations,
The tale of others' sufferings seem.
Oh ! when the heart is freshly bleeding,
How longs it for that time to be,
When, through the mist of years receding,
Its woes but live in reverie !

And it can dwell on moonlight glimmer,
On evening shade and loneliness;
And, while the sky grows dim and dimmer,
Feel no untold and strange distress-
Only a deeper impulse given
By lonely hour and darkened room,
To solemn thoughts that soar to heaven,
Seeking a life and world to come.

There Is Pleasure In The Pathless Woods by Lord Byron
There is a pleasure in the pathless woods,
There is a rapture on the lonely shore,
There is society, where none intrudes,
By the deep sea, and music in its roar:
I love not man the less, but Nature more,
From these our interviews, in which I steal
From all I may be, or have been before,
To mingle with the Universe, and feel
What I can ne'er express, yet cannot all conceal.

She Walks In Beauty by Lord Byron
She walks in Beauty, like the night
Of cloudless climes and starry skies;
And all that's best of dark and bright
Meet in her aspect and her eyes:
Thus mellowed to that tender light
Which Heaven to gaudy day denies.

One shade the more, one ray the less,
Had half impaired the nameless grace
Which waves in every raven tress,
Or softly lightens o'er her face;
Where thoughts serenely sweet express,
How pure, how dear their dwelling-place.

And on that cheek, and o'er that brow,
So soft, so calm, yet eloquent,

The smiles that win, the tints that glow,
But tell of days in goodness spent,
A mind at peace with all below,
A heart whose love is innocent!

The Ship Of Death by DH Lawrence

I
Now it is autumn and the falling fruit
and the long journey towards oblivion.

The apples falling like great drops of dew
to bruise themselves an exit from themselves.

And it is time to go, to bid farewell
to one's own self, and find an exit
from the fallen self.

II
Have you built your ship of death, O have you?
O build your ship of death, for you will need it.

The grim frost is at hand, when the apples will fall
thick, almost thundrous, on the hardened earth.

And death is on the air like a smell of ashes!
Ah! can't you smell it?

And in the bruised body, the frightened soul
finds itself shrinking, wincing from the cold
hat blows upon it through the orifices.

III
And can a man his own quietus make
with a bare bodkin?

With daggers, bodkins, bullets, man can make
a bruise or break of exit for his life;
but is that a quietus, O tell me, is it quietus?

Surely not so! for how could murder, even self-murder
ever a quietus make?

IV
O let us talk of quiet that we know,
that we can know, the deep and lovely quiet
of a strong heart at peace!

How can we this, our own quietus, make?

V
Build then the ship of death, for you must take

the longest journey, to oblivion.

And die the death, the long and painful death
that lies between the old self and the new.

Already our bodies are fallen, bruised, badly bruised,
already our souls are oozing through the exit
of the cruel bruise.

Already the dark and endless ocean of the end
is washing in through the breaches of our wounds,
already the flood is upon us.

Oh build your ship of death, your little ark
and furnish it with food, with little cakes, and wine
for the dark flight down oblivion.

VI
Piecemeal the body dies, and the timid soul
has her footing washed away, as the dark flood rises.

We are dying, we are dying, we are all of us dying
and nothing will stay the death-flood rising within us
and soon it will rise on the world, on the outside world.

We are dying, we are dying, piecemeal our bodies are dying
and our strength leaves us,
and our soul cowers naked in the dark rain over the flood,
cowering in the last branches of the tree of our life.

VII
We are dying, we are dying, so all we can do
is now to be willing to die, and to build the ship
of death to carry the soul on the longest journey.

A little ship, with oars and food
and little dishes, and all accoutrements
fitting and ready for the departing soul.

Now launch the small ship, now as the body dies
and life departs, launch out, the fragile soul
in the fragile ship of courage, the ark of faith
with its store of food and little cooking pans
and change of clothes,
upon the flood's black waste
upon the waters of the end
upon the sea of death, where still we sail
darkly, for we cannot steer, and have no port.

There is no port, there is nowhere to go
only the deepening black darkening still
blacker upon the soundless, ungurgling flood

darkness at one with darkness, up and down
and sideways utterly dark, so there is no direction any more
and the little ship is there; yet she is gone.
She is not seen, for there is nothing to see her by.
She is gone! gone! and yet
somewhere she is there.
Nowhere!

VIII
And everything is gone, the body is gone
completely under, gone, entirely gone.
The upper darkness is heavy as the lower,
between them the little ship
is gone
she is gone.

It is the end, it is oblivion.

IX
And yet out of eternity a thread
separates itself on the blackness,
a horizontal thread
that fumes a little with pallor upon the dark.

Is it illusion? or does the pallor fume
A little higher?
Ah wait, wait, for there's the dawn,
the cruel dawn of coming back to life out of oblivion.

Wait, wait, the little ship
drifting, beneath the deathly ashy grey of a flood-dawn.

Wait, wait! even so, a flush of yellow
and strangely, O chilled wan soul, a flush of rose.

A flush of rose, and the whole thing starts again.

X
The flood subsides, and the body, like a worn sea-shell
emerges strange and lovely.
And the little ship wings home, faltering and lapsing on the pink flood,

and the frail soul steps out, into the house again
filling the heart with peace.

Swings the heart renewed with peace even of oblivion.

Oh build your ship of death, oh build it!
for you will need it.
For the voyage of oblivion awaits you.

Afternoon in School The Last Lesson by DH Lawrence
When will the bell ring, and end this weariness?
How long have they tugged the leash, and strained apart
My pack of unruly hounds: I cannot start
Them again on a quarry of knowledge they hate to hunt,
I can haul them and urge them no more.
No more can I endure to bear the brunt
Of the books that lie out on the desks: a full three score
Of several insults of blotted pages and scrawl
Of slovenly work that they have offered me.
I am sick, and tired more than any thrall
Upon the woodstacks working weariedly.

And shall I take
The last dear fuel and heap it on my soul
Till I rouse my will like a fire to consume
Their dross of indifference, and burn the scroll
Of their insults in punishment? - I will not!
I will not waste myself to embers for them,
Not all for them shall the fires of my life be hot,
For myself a heap of ashes of weariness, till sleep
Shall have raked the embers clear: I will keep
Some of my strength for myself, for if I should sell
It all for them, I should hate them -
- I will sit and wait for the bell.

www.ingramcontent.com/pod-product-compliance
Lightning Source LLC
Chambersburg PA
CBHW060132050426
42448CB00010B/2093